SLEEP DISORDERS

THE ENCYCLOPEDIA OF PSYCHOLOGICAL DISORDERS

Senior Consulting Editor Carol C. Nadelson, M.D.
Consulting Editor Claire E. Reinburg

SLEEP DISORDERS

Linda Bayer

CHELSEA HOUSE PUBLISHERS
Philadelphia

This book is dedicated to Col. James R. McDonough, whose wisdom, compassion, and humanity are as apparent in his writing as they are abundant in his work. McDonough's classic depiction of war's nightmare also preserves dreams of love and peace. In literature, as in life, he leads by example and catches the essence out of the corner of his eye. The measure of the man is the way he treats subordinates.

The ENCYCLOPEDIA OF PSYCHOLOGICAL DISORDERS provides up-to-date information on the history of, causes and effects of, and treatment and therapies for problems affecting the human mind. The titles in this series are not intended to take the place of the professional advice of a psychiatrist or mental health care professional.

Chelsea House Publishers
Editor in Chief: Stephen Reginald
Production Manager: Pamela Loos
Art Director: Sara Davis
Director of Photography: Judy L. Hasday
Managing Editor: James D. Gallagher
Senior Production Editor: J. Christopher Higgins

Staff for SLEEP DISORDERS
Prepared by P. M. Gordon Associates, Philadelphia
Picture Researcher: P. M. Gordon Associates
Associate Art Director: Takeshi Takahashi
Cover Designer: Emiliano Begnardi

The Chelsea House World Wide Web address is
http://www.chelseahouse.com

First Printing

9 8 7 6 5 4 3 2 1

Library of Congress Cataloging-in-Publication Data

Bayer, Linda N.
Sleep disorders / by Dr. Linda Bayer.
   p.   cm. —(Encyclopedia of Psychological Disorders)
Includes bibliographical references and index.
Summary: Examines various sleep disorders, including primary insomnia, primary hypersomnia, narcolepsy, breathing-related sleep disorder, circadian rhythm sleep disorder, nightmares, and sleepwalking.
ISBN 0-7910-5314-8 (hc)
1. Sleep disorders—Juvenile literature. [1. Sleep disorders. 2. Sleep.]
I. Title. II. Series.
RC547.B395 2000
616.8'498—dc21   99-28882
                                                                      CIP

CONTENTS

PSYCHOLOGICAL DISORDERS AND THEIR EFFECT

CAROL C. NADELSON, M.D.
PRESIDENT AND CHIEF EXECUTIVE OFFICER,
The American Psychiatric Press

There are a wide range of problems that are considered psychological disorders, including mental and emotional disorders, problems related to alcohol and drug abuse, and some diseases that cause both emotional and physical symptoms. Psychological disorders often begin in early childhood, but during adolescence we see a sharp increase in the number of people affected by these disorders. It has been estimated that about 20 percent of the U.S. population will have some form of mental disorder sometime during their lifetime. Some psychological disorders appear following severe stress or trauma. Others appear to occur more often in some families and may have a genetic or inherited component. Still other disorders do not seem to be connected to any cause we can yet identify. There has been a great deal of attention paid to learning about the causes and treatments of these disorders, and exciting new research has taught us a great deal in the past few decades.

The fact that many new and successful treatments are available makes it especially important that we reject old prejudices and outmoded ideas that consider mental disorders to be untreatable. If psychological problems are identified early, it is possible to prevent serious conse-quences. We should not keep these problems hidden or feel shame that we or a member of our family has a mental disorder. Some people believe that something they said or did caused a mental disorder. Some people think that these disorders are "only in your head" so that you could "snap out of it" if you made the effort. This type of thinking implies that a treatment is a matter of willpower or motivation. It is a terrible burden for someone who is suffering to be blamed for his or her misery, and often people with psychological disorders are not treated compassionately. We hope that the information in this book will teach you about various mental illnesses.

The problems covered in the volumes in the ENCYCLOPEDIA OF PSYCHOLOGICAL DISORDERS were selected because they are of particular importance to young adults, because they affect them directly or because they affect family and friends. There are individual volumes on reading disorders, attention-deficit and disruptive behavior disorders, and dementia—all of these are related to our abilities to learn and integrate information from the world around us. There are books on drug abuse that provide useful information about the effects of these drugs and treatments that are available for those individuals who have drug problems. Some of the books concentrate on one of the most common mental disorders, depression. Others deal with eating disorders, which are dangerous illnesses that affect a large number of young adults, especially women.

Most of the public attention paid to these disorders arises from a particular incident involving a celebrity that awakens us to our own vulnerability to psychological problems. These incidents of celebrities or public figures revealing their own psychological problems can also enable us to think about what we can do to prevent and treat these types of problems.

Most people take for granted the ability to sleep peacefully as this woman is doing. For many other individuals, however, achieving restful sleep is a constant struggle.

SLEEP DISORDERS: AN OVERVIEW

Every night, more than 100 million Americans struggle with sleep problems: Some people can't get to sleep, some sleep too much, and others suffer from a mixed-up pattern of sleeping and waking. Those who are able to fall asleep may experience disturbances such as sleepwalking, night terrors, breathing difficulties, snoring, or restless movements of their arms or legs. In fact, there are at least 84 different sleeping and waking disorders that can interfere with sleep— some of them serious enough to cause sufferers major problems with school, work, and relationships. These conditions can even be dangerous, since exhaustion caused by sleep problems increases the risk of involvement in traffic, industrial, and other accidents.

This volume of the ENCYCLOPEDIA OF PSYCHOLOGICAL DISORDERS explores the way that sleep works, the kinds of problems that can interfere with sleep, and the types of treatments that are available for those with sleep disturbances. Many different kinds of health care professionals—ranging from family practitioners, pediatricians, and neurologists to psychiatrists and psychologists—are qualified to diagnose and treat such problems. And, increasingly, organizations such as the American Academy of Sleep Medicine in Rochester, Minnesota, are being founded to boost awareness of these disorders.

For those who have only occasional difficulty falling asleep, there should be no cause for alarm. However, when a sleep problem creates considerable distress in a person's life, the condition can and should be treated. An individual who suffers for more than a month from a sleep disturbance that interferes with his or her everyday life should consult a doctor or other health care provider. More serious problems may be referred to sleep disorders specialists. With the rapid development of the field of sleep medicine, these disorders are increasingly being identified and treated successfully.

The amount and kind of sleep that we need changes with age. As this pair slumbers, for example, the child will engage in longer periods of deeper sleep than his father.

1

INTRODUCTION TO SLEEP

On average, people spend about a third of their time asleep. This means that, by the time you reach your ninetieth birthday, chances are you will have spent about 30 years of your life in the Land of Nod. Yet most people know little about the process and importance of sleep.

In fact, only in the past 60 years have scientists come to understand something about what goes on in the brain at rest. With the invention of the *electro-encephalograph* (*EEG*), researchers were finally able to measure the electrical activity of the sleeping brain. The recordings of the EEG confirmed that different types of brain waves are produced during sleep.

Researchers can now trace the ebb and flow of our brain wave patterns as we drift into deep sleep. When we close our eyes and nod off, we move back and forth between quiet sleep and deeper, active sleep all night long. We go through four or five 90- to 110-minute rounds of this basic quiet-active sleep cycle each night.

QUIET SLEEP

During quiet sleep our body functions begin to slow down, and our brain waves become irregular. There are four stages of quiet sleep:

Stage One: As we close our eyes and drift off, we enter Stage One, which lasts for only a few minutes. Our muscles start to relax as our heart rate and brain waves begin to slow down and become irregular. At this point, we are still vaguely aware of what's going on around us. Typically, when we are awakened at this point, we will deny that we were sleeping.

Stage Two: Our bodies continue to slow down as our thoughts become more disorganized. We are no longer aware of our surroundings, but at this stage we can still be awakened easily. After lingering in Stage Two for 5 to 20 minutes, we drift into deeper sleep.

Stages Three and Four: Also known as delta sleep or slow-wave sleep, these phases are characterized by the deep unconscious state of the brain, by relaxed muscles, and by slowed body functions. It's much more difficult to awaken from this level of sleep than from the previous stages. As we move from Stage Three to Stage Four, our sleep continues to deepen. Slow-wave sleep is considered crucial to a feeling of well-being upon awakening. Research shows that, no matter how much time we spend in the first two stages of sleep, if we lack sufficient slow-wave sleep, we feel tired the next day. For this reason, people who are prevented from entering deep sleep because they are continually awakened during the night do not feel rested the following day.

ACTIVE SLEEP

By watching the movement of a person's eyes beneath closed eyelids, we can tell when the individual has entered active sleep. This rapid eye movement (REM) is the signal that the person's body metabolism has speeded up. At the same time, the brain begins to produce distinctive wave patterns.

REM sleep, which lasts about 10 minutes, is the time when most dreaming takes place. If we awaken someone during REM sleep, nearly 80 percent of the time the person will be able to recall very vivid dreams. But the same individual, awakened during quiet sleep, will remember his or her dreams only about 10 percent of the time. It's not surprising, then, that REM sleep is also known as "dream sleep."

CYCLES AND RHYTHMS

This explains the process of sleep, but what about its cause? Why do we fall asleep in the first place? The answer to this question involves an incredibly complex interaction between humans and their environment that is closely linked to our own internal rhythms and cycles.

Internal mechanisms that control our biological rhythms follow a 25-hour cycle known as the circadian rhythm, from the Latin words *circa* (about) and *dies* (day). Biological rhythms (sometimes called biological clocks) are physiological systems that allow us to live in harmony with the rhythms of nature, such as the cycles of day and night. Our bodies also follow a daily temperature cycle that is tied to sleep patterns, with long periods of sleep usually starting when our body temperature is lowest. From an evolutionary standpoint, sleep saves energy, because it allows humans and other animals to go without eating and run on less fuel for a longer period of time.

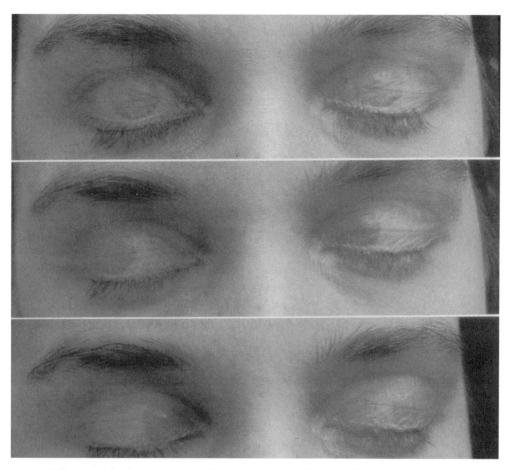

Active sleep, also known as dream sleep, is characterized by the rapid eye movement shown in this photo.

A HISTORY OF SLEEP AND DREAMS

Sleep and dreams have fascinated humanity since well before people understood anything about the process. In the ancient world, dreams were often regarded as prophetic visions of the future. In the Bible, for example, Joseph's interpretation of the Pharaoh's dreams allowed him to stockpile food in preparation for upcoming shortages in Egypt. In the twentieth century, Freud interpreted the symbols he found in his patients' dreams in order to uncover information about their secret fears and wishes. In modern art, surrealism expanded on romanticism's fascination with dreams. From every country, a wide array of artists—

Since ancient times, dreams have held a special attraction for people. In this illustration, for example, the artist depicts the Bible story in which Joseph interprets the Pharaoh's dream.

including the Spanish painter Salvador Dali, the Russian-American artist Marc Chagall, the Belgian painter René Magritte, and the Italian-Greek artist Giorgio de Chirico—depicted the irrational, whimsical land of dreams, where cows fly, clocks melt, apples fill entire rooms, and mannequins hold court. When Dali awakened from fitful slumber during the night, he would try to capture his nightmares on canvas before his mind had a chance to leave behind the land of dreams.

A similar attraction to dreamlike images is evident in modern literature. Poetry, drama, novels, and short stories abound in which dream sequences replace waking consciousness. British poet Samuel Coleridge and American poet and short-story writer Edgar Allan Poe—followed by Czech novelist Franz Kafka and Colombian author Gabriel García Márquez—were among scores of great writers around the world who portrayed dreamlike states where fantasy and nightmare traverse the domain of drug states, dreams, aimless musing, and fear.

Only recently, however, have we begun to understand the importance of sleep and dreams in our daily lives.

OUR NEED FOR SLEEP

We know that getting enough sleep improves our moods and our efficiency in school, on the job, and at home. However, the exact amount of sleep we need and the type of sleep we experience change according to our age and stage of development. During the first year of life, children spend most of their time in REM sleep. In young children,

GET A GOOD NIGHT'S SLEEP!

When we develop good sleep habits, we become more alert, healthier, and better able to fend off infections. Here are some simple rules to follow:

- Avoid drinking alcohol within several hours of bedtime (or when you're sleepy).
- Avoid eating or drinking anything with caffeine within six hours of bedtime.
- Avoid smoking, especially near bedtime.
- Avoid taking sleeping pills (and never combine alcohol with sleeping pills).
- Exercise during the day but not within six hours of bedtime.
- Get out of bed at about the same time each day.
- Go to bed only when you're sleepy.
- Keep a regular schedule for eating meals, doing chores, and taking medications.
- Set up a relaxing bedtime ritual (for example, take a hot bath or read for a few minutes).

The rapid growth that typically occurs during adolescence produces an increased demand for sleep. This groggy teen is showing the effects of the conflict between his need for more sleep and his daily school and social schedule.

periods of deeper sleep are still more abundant than in adulthood. Then, during the preschool and school-age years, the amount of sleep needed gradually decreases. In an article entitled "Pediatric Sleep Disorders," Thomas Anders and Lisa Eiben point out, however, that during the teen years the body demands more and more sleep. One of the primary reasons for this, experts believe, is that adolescence is typically a period of rapid growth, and the body produces most of its growth hormone during sleep. Because this increased need for sleep can often conflict with school demands and social life, it's not surprising that teens frequently appear to be unrested. Then, as we enter adulthood, the depth and continuity of our sleep diminishes. In later years, increased wakefulness during Stage One may make it harder to fall asleep, and Stages Three and Four become shorter. This is why older people tend to awaken early.

Because people had little understanding of sleep before technology began to reveal its complexity and purpose, some individuals dismissed its importance and helped create a culture in which sleep deprivation became widespread. Thomas Edison, who revolutionized the world by creating more than 1,300 inventions, dismissed sleep as "unproductive." Edison thought sleep was a bad habit that should be done away with. "For myself, I never found need of more than four or five hours' sleep in the twenty-four," Edison stated. If he slept more than that, he claimed, he would wake up feeling dull and lazy. Edison even wrote that he believed that long hours of sleep produced lower intelligence. So strongly did he value wakefulness that he hoped that, when darkness was banished through the use of his lightbulbs, the need for sleep would disappear.

In fact, it is true that the average amount of time people sleep has dropped from nine hours in the pre–lightbulb era to seven and a half hours today. However, for most of us, lack of sleep does not (as Edison implied) improve our mental abilities. On the contrary, it interferes with clear thinking and reduces efficiency. Each year, sleep-related errors and accidents cost U.S. businesses an estimated $56 billion, cause nearly 25,000 deaths, and result in 2.5 million disabling injuries.

We now know that higher thought processes depend on sleep so that information can be processed and stored in some way. People who are deprived of sleep for four or five days in a row typically begin to exhibit paranoia (feelings of persecution) and other signs of mental instability. Getting a good night's sleep is also important because sleep is a sort of "time out" that allows our brains and bodies to recharge. At the same time, our bodies circulate vitamins, minerals, and hormones and produce infection-fighting substances. (This is why parents insist on bed rest when their children are fighting off a cold.)

Edison may well have been able to get by on little sleep, but each person has his or her own distinct sleep needs. Infants sleep about 18 hours a day and adults can get by with about six or seven. Our own sleep requirements may vary from day to day, but we can tell we're getting enough sleep if we wake up feeling refreshed and can stay alert all day.

Unfortunately, we don't always get a good night's sleep. If such dis-

Thomas Alva Edison, shown here in his New Jersey laboratory, launched more than the age of modern electronics with his development of the first electric lightbulb. Before the invention of the lightbulb, people slept an average of nine hours a night. Today a typical night's sleep consists of only seven and a half hours.

turbances become problematic, *polysomnography*—a sleep-monitoring test—can be used to diagnose the difficulty. Polysomnography, which measures EEG activity to monitor the stages of sleep, uses the following standard measurements to facilitate the diagnosis of sleep disorders: *sleep latency*, the amount of time a person requires to fall asleep; *sleep continuity*, the overall balance of an individual's sleep and wakefulness throughout the night (better sleep occurs when interruption is minimized); *intermittent wakefulness*, the amount of wakefulness that takes place after the onset of initial sleep; *sleep efficacy*, the ratio of actual minutes spent asleep relative to the time spent in bed (higher numbers indicate better sleep); and *sleep architecture*, the number and distribution of sleep stages. A person who has been experiencing sleep problems (too much sleep or too little sleep) for more than a month and who finds that the condition is interfering with his or her life should see a doctor or ask for a referral to a sleep disorders specialist.

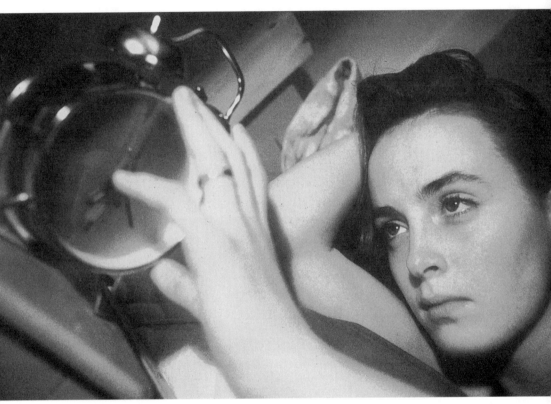

Many people have occasional difficulty getting to sleep. For individuals with insomnia, however, the problem is chronic, and it seriously disrupts their lives. Here a woman checks the clock after a long, sleepless night.

2

INSOMNIA

In his book *Sleep Thieves*, Stanley Coren claims that because of the importance of slumber, nature has gone to great lengths to ensure that its creatures have the ability to sleep. Some birds, for example, sleep during flight; some fish sleep as they swim; and some animals sleep with only half of the brain, using the other half to perform the functions necessary to keep them alive. Sometimes, however, nature's slumber mechanism can go awry, and we just can't get to sleep.

Insomnia refers to the inability to fall or stay asleep or the inability to sleep restfully. Not every difficulty falling asleep necessarily indicates insomnia, however. If an individual tosses and turns for a night or two because of concern about getting a project completed, he or she is probably not experiencing insomnia. Sleeping problems can also develop as a result of some diseases, depression, or the use of drugs such as cocaine, but these conditions are not considered true insomnia. A diagnosis of insomnia applies only if the symptoms cannot be attributed to these causes and only if they last for at least a month and cause the sufferer significant distress.

With insomnia, the quality of sleep and the perception of how much time is spent asleep are more important than the actual number of hours slept. Some people who suffer from insomnia have a history of being "light sleepers." For these individuals, noise and other interruptions easily disturb their slumber. As the sleep disturbances continue and fatigue increases, social or job problems can develop. A vicious cycle of sleeplessness can begin when a person with this condition feels wide awake at night and tries repeatedly to fall asleep. The more the individual attempts to sleep, the more frustrated he or she may become. Lying in bed awake night after night can condition the person to expect, and therefore increase the chances of, sleeplessness. Fatigue may cause the individual to fall asleep more and more often while watching television,

The physical requirement for sleep can produce considerable resourcefulness on the part of members of the animal kingdom. This black bear, for example, makes its snowy bed in the crook of a large tree.

reading, or riding in a car. Pretty soon, the person is sleeping better everywhere *except* in his or her own bed.

Insomnia is quite common. Approximately 36 out of every 100 Americans have reported experiencing this symptom. However, only 5 out of every 100 Americans consider the problem severe enough to seek medical help. Insomnia can be aggravated by bad sleep habits—for example, napping frequently during the day, keeping irregular hours, or working very late. But not everyone who gets little sleep suffers from insomnia.

Some people, like Edison, just naturally require less sleep. Such "short sleepers" seem to be able to get by on fewer hours of sleep than the rest of us can. These individuals don't suffer from insomnia, because the lack of sleep does not cause them distress. Researchers believe that the tendency to need little sleep may have a hereditary component.

TYPES OF INSOMNIA

There are two kinds of true insomnia: temporary insomnia (which appears in response to a problem or stress) and chronic insomnia (which develops into an ongoing problem that lasts six months or more).

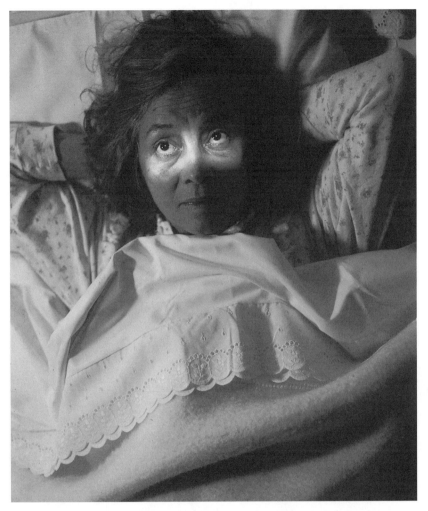

When light sleepers have repeated difficulty filtering out noise and other disturbances, the condition can lead to insomnia. The longer this woman has trouble sleeping each night, for example, the more she will expect sleeplessness and the greater chance she will have of experiencing insomnia.

TEMPORARY INSOMNIA

A sudden attack of insomnia can result from psychological or social stress or from physical pain. This is actually a normal response to stress. The sleeping problem may last for a number of weeks and then disappear. Because it is temporary, this form of insomnia usually doesn't require treatment. Individuals who are particularly sensitive to stress are more likely to respond to crises by losing sleep and by developing other symptoms, such as tension headaches and stomach distress. When insomnia persists long after the crisis has passed, however, the sleep problem may become chronic.

CHRONIC INSOMNIA

People with chronic insomnia typically feel generally run-down during the day. Having to endure this extended malaise can lead to depression, lack of motivation, and poor concentration. Individuals who don't sleep well at night and thus feel fatigued during the day sometimes try to compensate by drinking large amounts of coffee or by using other stimulants, such as amphetamines. This response can begin a cycle of drug abuse that involves taking amphetamines to stay awake during the day and taking barbiturates or other sleeping pills to offset the stimulants at night.

Chronic insomnia causes a general feeling of fatigue during the daytime. In this scene from the movie Dream for an Insomniac, *for example, Ione Skye—who plays a young woman who hasn't slept a full night since the age of six—stretches out on the couch during a conversation with friends.*

Although chronic insomnia can affect both young and old, young adults often report having trouble falling asleep, whereas older people more frequently complain of difficulty staying asleep.

TREATMENT

In order to treat insomnia, it's important to determine the type of problem and its cause. After a careful interview, a doctor may recommend special tests at a sleep clinic, which can help pinpoint the nature and degree of the insomnia.

A number of chemical substances have been prescribed to help people fall asleep more quickly, sleep more deeply, or stay asleep longer. The problem with using these products on a continuing basis, however, is that most are habit forming, have side effects, or both. In addition, more and more of the substance may be needed as the person builds up a tolerance for the drug, and it can become nearly impossible to sleep without it. For example, sleeping pills can interfere with the body's ability to produce or use the chemicals needed for sleep, and they can interfere with alertness or concentration during the day.

The best way to treat insomnia is to try to regain control of sleep. Typical methods include restricting the amount of time the person stays in bed; improving sleep habits, such as keeping regular hours; and decreasing or eliminating the use of medications (always under a doctor's care). Health care professionals may ask the patient to keep a "sleep diary" for two weeks. The individual will record his or her sleeping pattern and log details such as bedtime, amount of time required to fall asleep, number of times awakened during the night, and time of awakening. The patient may then be limited to a small amount of time in bed during a 24-hour period to trigger a mild kind of sleep deprivation, which can lead to better, more refreshed sleep.

Research has shown that a combination of *behavioral therapy*—such as the sleep diary/deprivation method—medication, and sometimes psychological counseling can help ease insomnia better than can medication alone. Behavioral therapy uses reinforcement to encourage desirable behaviors and discourage undesirable behaviors. Medication can be used to provide immediate relief until the patient learns relaxation and behavioral therapy techniques. Drug therapy should be gradually decreased as the individual applies new methods of sleep control.

People with hypersomnia or narcolepsy experience excessive sleepiness. This illustration depicts the daytime napping that becomes a compelling urge for individuals who suffer from these disturbances.

3
SLEEPINESS: HYPERSOMNIA AND NARCOLEPSY

J ust as there are some people who have trouble sleeping, there are those at the other end of the continuum who sleep too much. The condition known as *hypersomnia* is characterized by excessive sleepiness. *Narcolepsy*, a serious form of hypersomnia, is characterized by irresistible urges to sleep during the day, hallucinations (sensory perceptions in which a person imagines that something is real when it is not), and *sleep paralysis* (the inability to move shortly after awakening or shortly after dozing off). (See chapter 5 for a more detailed discussion of sleep paralysis.)

EXCESSIVE SLEEPINESS

When we talk about a person with hypersomnia, we don't mean simply that the person needs too much sleep. We mean that, although most people with this problem sleep 8 to 12 hours per night and the quality of their sleep is normal, they still have trouble waking up in the morning and feel sleepy during the day.

People with this condition typically experience excessive sleepiness for at least a month, and they fall asleep for long periods of time during the day on a regular basis. The need for too much sleep can cause significant stress and can interfere with school, work, and social relationships.

SYMPTOMS

People struggling with excessive sleepiness tend to fall asleep quickly and stay asleep for long periods of time. In addition, they sometimes experience the following:

- an argumentative attitude or grogginess on awakening
- excessive sleepiness for six months or more

Excessive sleepiness in individuals who drive or operate heavy machinery can be particularly dangerous. In these cases, tragedies such as this fatal school bus accident are frequently the result.

• extremely deep sleep
• gradual onset of the problem

Excessive sleepiness during the day can lead to "automatic behavior" in which a person who is engaging in a relatively routine activity, such as driving a car or walking, suddenly can't remember being conscious for some portion of the procedure. In addition, general memory may be poor during periods of sleepiness. Because a person with this problem never feels rested, he or she may take both intentional and inadvertent naps during the day. Although these daytime sleep periods may last for more than an hour, they do not make the person feel refreshed.

Falling asleep during the day can result in major or minor difficulties. Because dozing off is sometimes misinterpreted as boredom or laziness, it can cause problems at home or at school and can affect personal relationships. Sleeping in class can lead to disciplinary action by teachers or parents. Dozing off while operating heavy machinery or vehicles, on the other hand, can cause serious accidents and injuries. Nevertheless, sudden "sleep attacks" feel irresistible to people who suffer from hypersomnia. Typically these attacks occur in situations in which there is little stimulation and a low level of alertness. The person's concentration suffers as he or she tries to fight sleep.

HOW COMMON IS HYPERSOMNIA?

The prevalence of excessive sleepiness is not known. However, according to the fourth edition of the American Psychiatric Association's *Diagnostic and Statistical Manual of Disorders* (*DSM-IV*), it has been estimated that between 5 and 10 percent of those who seek help at sleep clinics suffer from this problem. The condition, which may be inherited, typically begins somewhere between the ages of 15 and 30 and gradually worsens. Without treatment, the problem does not usually improve.

People who suffer from hypersomnia should not be confused with "long sleepers," who simply need a lot of sleep. Unlike hypersomniacs, long sleepers feel refreshed, rather than sleepy or lethargic, once they have slept enough. People with hypersomnia feel drowsy no matter how much sleep they get.

People who simply haven't had enough sleep and try to catch up on their sleep during weekends, vacations, and other times when they are not required to get up at a fixed hour should be differentiated from hypersomniacs. For hypersomniacs, no amount of sleep allows them to catch up.

TREATMENT

The cause of excessive sleepiness is not fully understood. Therefore, treatment generally consists of changing behaviors—for example, keeping a regular bedtime and limiting afternoon naps to no more than one nap of no longer than 45 minutes. People who suffer from hypersomnia should avoid alcohol, caffeine, and night-shift work, and they should be sure to get at least eight and a half hours of sleep a night.

NARCOLEPSY

Narcolepsy is one of the most common types of hypersomnia. No matter how much a person with this condition rests, he or she will feel an irresistible need to sleep. Narcolepsy is a disabling brain disorder that affects the control of sleep and wakefulness. People who suffer from narcolepsy may fall asleep at any time—while having a conversation, walking down the street, or driving a car. These "sleep attacks" can last from mere seconds to more than 30 minutes. During a sleep attack, the person may experience *cataplexy*, a sudden loss of muscle tone that lasts for a few seconds or minutes and that can be triggered by intense emotion such as laughter or anger.

WHAT IS NARCOLEPSY?

Narcolepsy is really just a sudden intrusion of the dreaming state of sleep (REM sleep) into a person's waking hours. Drowsiness generally decreases after a sleep attack, only to return several hours later. Although sleep attacks may take place daily over a period of three months or more, most people suffer from the disorder for years before seeking medical attention. In fact, according to the National Institutes of Health, only about 50,000 of the estimated 200,000 Americans with narcolepsy have been diagnosed.

SYMPTOMS

Although the initial symptoms of narcolepsy—daytime sleepiness and irresistible sleep attacks—usually appear during the late teens and early twenties, some researchers contend that narcolepsy can be present but go unrecognized during childhood. Onset after age 40 is unusual. Disrupted nighttime sleep usually develops later in the course of the disorder, perhaps when the individual enters middle age.

The classic symptoms of narcolepsy include

- cataplexy
- excessive daytime sleepiness
- hallucinations when falling asleep
- sleep paralysis

Other symptoms that sometimes appear involve nighttime sleep disturbances, including experiencing nightmares, having leg jerks, tossing and turning, and awakening frequently.

According to Anders and Eiben's "Pediatric Sleep Disorders," between

Cataplexy, daytime fatigue, hallucinations, and sleep paralysis are the classic symptoms of narcolepsy. But nightmares, leg jerks, restlessness, and frequent awakening can occur as well. This man is exhibiting the tossing and turning that can sometimes accompany the disorder.

0.07 and 0.04 percent of the population suffers from narcolepsy. This means that narcolepsy is twice as common as multiple sclerosis and half as common as Parkinson's disease. The precise cause of the illness is unknown, but scientists do know that genetic factors play a role. Experts believe that narcolepsy occurs when something in the environment triggers its development in a person with a biological predisposition to the condition. In 1999, Stanford University researchers identified one gene that causes narcolepsy, giving hope that it may someday be possible to design a drug to treat the disorder.

In about half the cases of narcolepsy, according to the *DSM-IV*, severe psychological stress or altered sleeping schedules herald the onset of the illness. About 40 percent of sufferers have a history of other

Use of the drug modafinil and psychological counseling have both been effective in the treatment of narcolepsy. Here a therapist helps family members gain an understanding of the disorder.

mental disorders. Some studies indicate that a history of sleepwalking, clenching the jaw and grinding teeth, and bed-wetting may be more common in people who have narcolepsy.

The *DSM-IV* estimates that, just before falling asleep or just after awakening, between 20 and 40 percent of people who suffer from narcolepsy experience hallucinations. Most of these are visual and incorporate elements of the environment, such as imaginary objects that come through real cracks in a wall. Some hallucinations involve sounds, such as hearing burglars who are not really there. Other hallucinations involve the sensation of flying.

In addition, according to the *DSM-IV*, just before falling asleep or just after awakening between 30 and 50 percent of narcoleptics experience sleep paralysis, making them unable to speak or move. Although the diaphragm is not paralyzed and they continue to breathe, some of these individuals complain that they experience difficulty breathing. Sleep paralysis can also occur during the blurred boundary between sleep and wakefulness that is commonly prolonged for narcoleptics as they emerge from REM sleep.

Although sleep-related hallucinations and paralysis generally last only a few seconds or minutes, the symptoms—especially when they occur together—can be quite terrifying.

TREATMENT

The drug modafinil, which was approved to treat narcolepsy in December 1998 and became available by prescription in February 1999, was the first drug developed in 40 years specifically for excessive daytime sleepiness and narcolepsy. Although this medication promotes wakefulness, it does not stimulate the rest of the body or cause anxiety or irritability. Moreover, it is not highly addictive, as are so many stimulants and antidepressants that have been used to treat narcolepsy in the past and that typically reduce, rather than alleviate, symptoms.

Counseling may also help people adjust to this chronic, lifelong ailment. Some of the symptoms may diminish over time. Keeping a regular bedtime and taking a few scheduled half-hour naps throughout the day can bring some relief. It may sometimes be necessary to adjust school and work routines to accommodate the need for more sleep. Family therapy can help other members of the household understand the problem and its constraints.

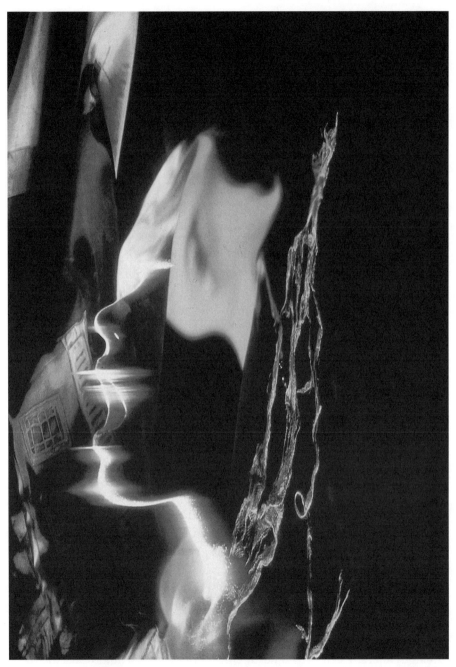

Nightmares and night terrors can both be extremely frightening to those who experience them. However, screaming—depicted in this digital art by Sergio Duarte—is more likely to accompany night terrors than nightmares.

4

NIGHTMARES AND
NIGHT TERRORS

Nightmares and night terrors are very frightening dreams that can cause considerable distress. The major difference between nightmares and night terrors is that nightmares occur only during REM (dreaming) sleep and can begin at any time during the night, but night terrors take place during the first three hours of sleep, during a nondreaming period. In addition, people can be awakened by, or from, a nightmare and can often remember all too well what they were dreaming. When individuals have night terrors, on the other hand, they are very difficult to awaken and typically remember little or nothing of what they were dreaming or what they feared.

NIGHTMARES

A HISTORY

In many ancient cultures, dreams and nightmares were viewed as messages from the gods or as predictions of the future. The Sumerians and Babylonians in Mesopotamia, as well as the Egyptians, Israelites, and Greeks, often regarded nightmares as omens from a divine source, warning people about impending evil. In this animistic world, in which spirits—including devils and demons—controlled events in unpredictable ways, being in communication with the gods was considered essential. Many Babylonian and Assyrian dream books were collected in a library at the ancient Assyrian capital of Nineveh.

In ancient Egypt, a statuette of a dead person and a list of his or her good deeds was tied to the wrist of the living spouse to cure him or her of being tormented in nightmares by the deceased. The ancient Greeks practiced dream incubation, a process designed to encourage dreams, which were then subject to interpretation. People slept in temples after fasting, praying, or making other preparations for the dreams they would have that night.

This practice can perhaps be traced to sleeping on graves in order to receive ghostly messages from the dead. In the *Iliad*, the Greek poet Homer speaks of people lying on earthen beds in order to receive prophetic dreams, and the Greek historian Herodotus (fifth century B.C.) wrote that people "slept on the graves of their ancestors in order to have dreams." It is not surprising that bad dreams and nightmares were often evoked while sleeping atop graves. Eventually, sacred places such as remote hillsides, caverns, gorges, streams, or temples near cities became the locations for dream incubation. Dream temples, with labyrinthine structures that the incubant entered before going to sleep, were often part of the larger temple complex.

Throughout history, people have been fascinated with dreams and nightmares as alternative forms of consciousness. Psychoanalyst Sigmund Freud thought dreams were a form of wish fulfillment that served the individual's psychological needs. Whereas Freud interpreted all types of dreams as expressions of the individual's own mind and personality, Swiss psychologist Carl Jung considered dreams a reflection of a collective unconscious shared by an entire society and developed over eons. Jung believed that, by providing a connection between the conscious and subconscious parts of the mind that allow the person to stay in balance emotionally, dreams help people remain psychologically healthy. Through dreams, he believed, the unconscious can send messages to the conscious self.

SYMPTOMS

A nightmare typically involves a lengthy, elaborate dream sequence. Such frightening dreams may follow traumatic experiences, or they may appear for what seems like no reason at all. Nightmares take place almost exclusively during REM (dreaming) sleep and typically occur very late at night. They frequently deal with imminent physical danger from pursuit, attack, or injury, which is extremely frightening to the dreamer. Less often, they involve more subtle threats, such as failure or embarrassment.

Although nightmares that follow traumatic events may repeat the terrifying experience, most nightmares don't recount actual events. Upon awakening, the dreamer can often recall the dream sequence in detail. Sometimes multiple nightmares that deal with the same theme take place during a single night. Nightmares end with awakening, and the dreamer generally regains full alertness immediately. Because fear and anxiety may persist, however, the individual may have difficulty returning to sleep.

Because the dreamer can often recall his or her nightmares, the individual may remain anxious for some time after awakening. This little girl, for instance, resists going back to sleep for fear that her nightmare will recur.

During a nightmare, a person may experience other symptoms, including a racing heart, sweating, and rapid breathing. However, because nightmares take place during deep REM sleep, when the body is more relaxed, body movements and screaming are not typical. When talking or screaming do occur, they often take place during the transition from sleep to wakefulness.

CAUSES

Nightmares are attributed to numerous causes. Children's nightmares, which often begin between three and six years of age, frequently reflect the struggle to deal with typical childhood fears and difficulties.

Nightmares are not uncommon in early childhood. In this illustration, for example, a little girl is dreaming about the objects that occupy her waking hours. Normal childhood fears could easily turn her imaginings into a nightmare.

Most children outgrow the problem. In some cases, however, nightmares persist and become a lifelong difficulty.

Many people suffer from nightmares after surviving or witnessing a traumatic event, such as a severe accident or the loss of a loved one. Because of the profoundly distressing experiences of combat, for example, recurrent nightmares often haunt war veterans. Sometimes these nightmares, which are usually directly related to the traumatic event, may not occur until months or years after the horrifying experience.

Some people experience nightmares when they face stressful situations or major changes in their lives. Many pregnant women, for example, suffer from nightmares that their babies will be deformed or stillborn. Still other individuals, usually those who are more emotional or sensitive, suffer from nightmares that seem totally unrelated to their waking lives.

Certain medical conditions, substance abuse, and high fevers can cause nightmares. Alcohol and drugs—including medications for high blood pressure; drugs of abuse such as amphetamines, cocaine, and other stimulants; and antidepressants—can bring on or repress nightmares. A small percentage of nightmares may be triggered by lesions on the brainstem or by central nervous system infections.

HOW COMMON ARE NIGHTMARES?

According to the *DSM-IV*, between 10 and 50 percent of youngsters three to five years of age have nightmares frightening enough to disturb their parents. Among adults, half the population has an occasional nightmare. More women than men report nightmares, but this may be because fearful reactions are more widely tolerated in women.

Not everyone who has ever had a nightmare suffers from a disorder, however. According to the *DSM-IV*, nightmares must be recurrent and greatly distressing for this diagnosis to be made.

BEHAVIORAL TREATMENT

When nightmares are chronic, however, two forms of behavioral treatment—rehearsal and desensitization—have been used with some success.

In desensitization, the therapist teaches the individual muscle relaxation techniques and asks him or her to write down descriptions of the frightening nightmares. Then the nightmare sufferer practices the relaxation techniques while reading through these notes, whenever he or she thinks about the bad dream, and at bedtime.

With rehearsal, the therapist instructs the patient to write a new ending for the nightmare or to change the course of terrifying aspects of the dream. In a relaxed state, the patient rehearses the revised nightmare—imagining the new version at least once a day, until the individual becomes used to the portions that he or she formerly found disturbing. The therapist may help create the new storyline for the nightmare and may also give the patient instruction on relaxation techniques. In group sessions, nightmare sufferers can recite their new dreams to each other. To further prevent the individual from feeling alone in confronting his or her problem, the therapist typically encourages the patient to telephone him or her if the bad dream recurs.

Some people have experienced dramatic improvement using these procedures. According to a 1992 article by Robert Kellner and associates in the *American Journal of Psychiatry*, one study found that, within 7 months of beginning behavioral treatments, 23 patients who had suffered from nightmares for more than 20 years reported a significant decrease in the dreams. There seemed to be no difference in results between those who were treated through rehearsal and those who were treated through densensitization.

■   ■   ■

CASE HISTORY

Mary was a 36-year-old woman who sought help from a psychologist because of a recurrent disturbing dream about her deceased father. Mary's father had suffered from multiple sclerosis, and his marriage to Mary's mother had been fraught with loud arguments and emotional pain. The family had been deeply affected by the chronic illness but had never discussed the problem. Despite the years of anger and disillusion, Mary's parents had not divorced. Instead, they had fought bitterly until her father's death.

In Mary's recurrent nightmare, her father was alive, but he had been divorced from her mother and had been living away from his family in a nursing home for many years. In the dream, Mary and her sister had stayed with their mother and had not seen their father after the divorce. As the dream opened, Mary was overcome with pain and remorse for having "abandoned" her father to the nursing home and for having failed to visit him there after the divorce. Mary reported to the psychologist that, despite the fact that none of these events had actually taken place, the pain and guilt were overwhelming in the nightmare. (Interestingly, Mary's sister reported similar recurring dreams, causing the same feelings of guilt and remorse, for many years.)

Mary's psychologist suggested that she "rehearse" a new ending for her dream. The therapist suggested that Mary revise the nightmare so that in the dream she discussed her feelings with her father. In this way she would change the outcome of the dream and avoid the deep-seated, searing pain it caused. The psychologist instructed Mary to imagine the new version of the dream every day.

It wasn't long before Mary's dream recurred. But this time, in the dream, she remembered the "rehearsal," and she carried out her plan. She sat down at the kitchen table with her father and confronted him, telling him just how the anger and arguments had affected her. Mary and her father had a wonderful conversation, and she woke up feeling peaceful and guilt free. She never had the nightmare again.

NIGHT TERRORS

According to Ernest Hartmann's *The Nightmare*, experiencing night terrors (also called sleep terrors, *pavor nocturnus*, or incubus attack) is a relatively common problem, occurring most frequently in young children between the ages of three and five. During an attack, the child will typically let out a panicky scream or cry of intense fear. Some children may sit up in bed, stand, or even run through the house, fighting an imaginary object or an attacker as if they are being threatened. Waking the child during a night terror can be quite difficult. Upon awakening the following morning, the child generally won't be able to remember anything about the episode.

Night terrors usually begin at about the same time every night, usually a few hours after the child has fallen asleep. Generally, only one night terror will occur during the night. Some individuals experience chronic night terrors, whereas others experience only one. When the problem persists, night terrors can be separated by days or weeks or can occur on consecutive nights.

During a typical attack, after abruptly sitting up in bed and screaming or crying, the child will display the following symptoms:

- dilated pupils
- flushed face

- perspiration
- racing heart beat
- racing pulse

If the child awakens, he or she will usually be confused and disoriented for several minutes. Generally, however, the youngster will not fully awaken and will go back to sleep. Embarrassment about night terrors may cause youngsters to refuse to attend overnight camp or sleepovers at friends' homes.

Sometimes (more commonly with adults than with children) the person awakening from a sleep terror may get up and run, punch another person, or try to defend him- or herself.

CAUSE

Most experts believe that night terrors are not caused by life situations, such as a bad day at school, a recent move, or parental divorce, although these events may aggravate the problem. Researchers believe that there may be a genetic component to the cause. A child whose parent had night terrors may have a greater chance of developing the condition. Fatigue may also play a role. Fever and sleep deprivation can both increase the frequency of night terrors.

It is believed, however, that night terrors are primarily the result of an immature developing brain that is struggling with the problem of moving from deep to light sleep. Caught in this sort of twilight zone of partial wakefulness and deep slumber, the child panics and responds with automatic defensive measures, such as screaming, crying, and thrashing around. According to this view, the child cannot recall a nightmare upon awakening, because no nightmare has occurred.

This theory would explain why the child who experiences a night terror can usually return to a peaceful sleep, without ever fully awakening, and has no memory of the frightening experience the following morning. It would also explain why most children outgrow night terrors by about age eight or nine, when the brain has developed the ability to switch between sleep stages and to regulate the various states of dreaming and sleeping.

Although it can be frightening to a parent who witnesses a child experiencing a night terror, the condition is generally not considered unusual or dangerous to the youngster. As the child's brain and sleep pattern mature, the terrors usually disappear.

HOW TO PREVENT NIGHT TERRORS

Because children who have night terrors usually experience them at about the same time each night, experts suggest the following preventive measures:

1. Awaken the child about 30 minutes before the night terror usually begins.
2. Get the youngster out of bed.
3. Talk to the child in a quiet, reassuring way, and encourage him or her to respond in kind.
4. Keep the youngster awake for at least five minutes.
5. Let the child go back to sleep.

Night terrors in children are neither unusual nor dangerous, and they usually disappear on their own over time. But some parents prefer to use preventive action rather than wait until the condition has run its course. This father, for example, awakens his son shortly before the time that the night terrors usually begin. Then he talks to him quietly and reassuringly and lets him go back to sleep.

HOW COMMON ARE NIGHT TERRORS?

Night terrors are most common in children, occurring more often in boys than in girls. The *DSM-IV* estimates that between 1 percent and 6 percent of all children experience these attacks. Night terrors are less common in adults (existing in under 1 percent of the population), and they occur equally in men and women.

In childhood, according to the *DSM-IV*, night terrors usually begin between the ages of 3 and 12 and decrease as adolescence approaches. In adults, the onset of night terrors is generally between the ages of 20 and 30.

Night terrors and sleepwalking (see chapter 5) tend to run in families. Although it is not known exactly how the problem is inherited, some studies indicate that the prevalence of the disease increases tenfold for people who have close relatives with either of these disorders.

■   ■   ■

CASE HISTORY

In *The Nightmare*, Dr. Hartmann reported the case of Josh, a seven-year-old boy whose parents were worried that he had been awakening at night in terror for the past few years. Josh's parents reported that the child was having "terrible nightmares from which we can't awaken him."

Half an hour to an hour after going to bed, Josh would sit up, scream, and then wander around "looking dazed and terrified." For five or ten minutes, Josh's parents would try to awaken him—often without success. When Josh finally awakened, he didn't seem to know where he was, but he appeared untroubled and returned to a quiet sleep for the rest of the night. Although Josh's parents spoke of his "nightmares," there was no evidence that Josh actually recalled a dream sequence. They were so upset by their son's attacks that they developed patterns of insomnia following Josh's sleep terrors. Interestingly, Josh's father had experienced sleepwalking episodes as a child.

Josh's night terrors often occurred on Saturday evenings. His doctor theorized that this was because on weekends Josh was allowed to stay up later than usual with his older brothers. By the second late night, Josh was tired—a condition that aggravates night terrors. Josh's doctor recommended family therapy to determine whether stress from a move, marital conflict or separation, or difficulties at school might be aggravating the problem. He emphasized the importance of creating a safe environment so that Josh would not encounter sharp objects, unlocked entry to the outdoors, or other risks until the sleepwalking and night terrors ceased.

TREATMENT

Most experts believe that, although night terrors frighten parents, they are not harmful to the child. Because of the danger of having a youngster get out of bed and wander around the house during a night terror, however, a child may need to be restrained during such attacks. Caretakers should not shout at or shake a child in the middle of a night terror. They should, instead, allow the episode to run its course. Anyone caring for the youngster—including baby-sitters, overnight camp counselors, and parents of friends having sleepovers—should be informed about the problem.

Because older children and adults who experience night terrors may worry about their mental stability, counseling can help reassure patients that these sleep problems can be controlled and that they are not a sign of insanity. At sleep clinics, doctors can test patients with night terrors and other sleep-related disorders in order to determine, and educate the patients about, irregularities that can occur during different phases of sleep. Polysomnographic printouts of electrical patterns produced by the brain during sleep can show the biological basis for sleep conditions and can help demystify the processes of sleep and dreaming.

Sleepwalking, also called somnambulism, occurs during the slow-wave stages of sleep. This time-lapse image shows a young woman as she sits up in bed, stands, and begins to walk in her sleep.

5

SLEEPWALKING AND OTHER SLEEP MOVEMENT CONDITIONS

SLEEPWALKING

Sleep problems don't all take place while a person is relaxing safely in bed. As we saw with night terrors, sleepwalking (or somnambulism) can manifest itself with other sleep conditions. It can also occur alone.

Sleepwalking is a series of complex behaviors that begin during slow-wave sleep and cause a sleeping person to get out of bed and walk around. Some people with this problem sleepwalk less than once a month, and they cause no one harm. Other individuals sleepwalk more than once a month but less than nightly. In its most severe form, sleepwalking takes place every night and can lead to injury.

Professional help is recommended for a sleepwalker who

- injures him- or herself while sleepwalking
- leaves the house while sleepwalking
- sleepwalks almost every night

In the mildest cases of sleepwalking, the person may not actually get out of bed. He or she may simply sit up, look around, and pick at the covers. More severe episodes will involve getting out of bed and moving around. During this time, the sleepwalker is typically unresponsive, maintaining a blank stare.

Most sleepwalkers remember little, if anything, about the experience. The individual may walk into closets, go up and down stairs, and even exit the building. While sleepwalking, a person can sometimes use the bathroom, eat, or even talk. A sleepwalker may run or make a frantic attempt to escape some imagined threat. Rarely, sleepwalkers have been known to unlock doors and operate machinery. Sleepwalking children may exhibit bizarre behavior, such as urinating in a closet. It can be difficult to awaken a sleepwalker, and, once awakened, the person is typically quite confused.

*When night terrors accompany sleepwalking, there is greater danger that the somnam-
bulist will harm him- or herself or others. Scott Falater, who murdered his wife by stab-
bing her 44 times and then drowning her, offered sleepwalking as a defense at his trial.
Here, Falater breaks down on the witness stand while testifying that he never would have
harmed his wife intentionally. The jury didn't believe him, however, and convicted him of
first-degree murder.*

Sleepwalking can be accompanied by sleep talking. The person may
make recognizable statements or speak in a garbled manner. Some individuals respond to questions while sleepwalking. However, their speech
is usually difficult to understand, and, when they awaken, they rarely
remember having spoken.

Typically, sleepwalking incidents last between several minutes and
half an hour. Sometimes sleepwalkers go to sleep in one bed and wake
up in another bed. They may find evidence of nighttime activities, such
as bits of uneaten food lying about, but they seldom remember what
happened.

WHAT CAN A SLEEPWALKER DO?

The following suggestions can be helpful to a sleepwalker:

- Avoid alcohol and sedatives.
- Don't go to bed with a full bladder.
- Follow a calming bedtime ritual, such as taking a warm bath, reading a book, or using relaxation or meditation techniques.
- Make sure you get plenty of rest (the more tired you are when you go to bed, the more likely it is that you will sleepwalk).
- Move your bedroom to the ground floor.
- Remove anything from the bedroom that could hurt you if you stumbled.
- Secure windows and doors.

Although children who sleepwalk usually outgrow the problem by the time they reach adolescence, the condition can recur in later years. This woman is attempting to control the disorder by creating a relaxing bedtime routine. Before she goes to sleep, she takes a warm bath, does relaxation exercises, and reads.

Researchers have not been able to pinpoint the causes of sleepwalking. However, they have noted a link between the tendency to suffer from migraine headaches, such as the man in this photo is experiencing, and the tendency to sleepwalk.

People who sleepwalk may avoid sleeping with partners and may hesitate to spend the night away from home. Although sleepwalking isn't dangerous in itself, sleepwalkers have been injured by inadvertently bumping into objects or falling down stairs. The risk of injuring oneself or others increases when night terrors are involved. In these cases, the individual may try to run away or strike out against imaginary attackers.

PREVALENCE

According to the *DSM-IV*, between 10 and 30 percent of children have experienced at least one episode of sleepwalking during their lives, but only 1 to 5 percent have a continuing problem with the condition. Between 1 and 7 percent of all men and women walk in their sleep. Violent episodes are more likely to occur among adult sleepwalkers.

Although experts don't understand what causes sleepwalking, they have discovered a connection between people who get migraine headaches and people who walk in their sleep. There also appears to be a genetic link—the *DSM-IV* reports that about 80 percent of sleepwalkers have relatives with the problem. When both parents are sleepwalkers, children have a 60 percent chance of developing the problem.

Sleepwalking can begin any time after a child learns to walk. According to the *DSM-IV*, however, the first incident usually takes place between 4 and 8 years of age, with frequency peaking at age 12. Rarely does the first instance of sleepwalking occur in adulthood. Usually, childhood sleepwalking disappears by adolescence (typically by age 15), but it can recur years later.

SLEEP PARALYSIS

By the 19th century, the phenomenon of sleep paralysis had been recorded. Sleep paralysis occurs when an individual feels entirely awake but unable to move, speak, or open his or her eyes for as long as ten seconds. The person may feel as though he or she is suffocating or may believe that someone is standing over the bed. This terrifying experience can occur alone or can accompany other symptoms, such as hallucinations.

Researchers—including N. E. Penn and associates; K. Fukuda and colleagues; G. B. Goode; and H. C. Everett—have provided results of different surveys of college and medical students. These surveys indicate that anywhere between 6 and 66 percent of the U.S. population have experienced at least one episode of sleep paralysis, some in association with narcolepsy. Articles written by J. U. Ohaeri and associates and C. C. Bell and colleagues suggest that isolated sleep paralysis typically begins in the twenties. Among people with narcolepsy it often occurs between ages 26 and 29. Research by M. Billiard and associates indicates that disrupted sleep, fatigue, stress, anxiety, or "hearty eating" may trigger sleep paralysis.

Isolated sleep paralysis and hallucinations are usually not severe enough to require treatment. Some medications seem to be effective for sleep paralysis, depression, and panic disorder (recurrent, unexpected panic attacks accompanied by worry about future attacks or by other behavioral changes). Another intervention involves having a witness touch the person and call his or her name or request that the individual move his or her eyes from side to side. It is helpful to reassure the person that the paralysis will not increase or become permanent. Individuals who suffer from narcolepsy may find that episodes of sleep paralysis and hallucinations cease to occur on their own, though it may take 12 or more years for them to do so.

TEETH GRINDING (BRUXISM)

Sleep *bruxism* is a type of movement disorder characterized by grinding or clenching the teeth during sleep. It is also known as nocturnal bruxism, nocturnal tooth grinding, and nocturnal tooth clenching. Some people experience occasional episodes of bruxism that do not harm the teeth or cause any other problems. Other individuals grind their teeth every night, which can damage the teeth and cause jaw disorders and other injuries.

SYMPTOMS

Symptoms include teeth grinding or clenching during sleep that can cause

- abnormal wear of the teeth
- jaw muscle discomfort
- unpleasant grinding noises

DIAGNOSIS

Tests for this condition reveal jaw muscle activity during sleep. Other sleep disorders, such as sleep *apnea* (periods of halted breathing), may occur at the same time. If tooth damage is not severe, a dentist can create a mouth guard that fits over the bottom teeth and prevents the top and bottom teeth from grinding against each other.

RESTLESS LEGS SYNDROME

Restless legs syndrome (RLS) is a condition characterized by a crawling, tingling, or prickly sensation in the legs that triggers an overwhelming urge to stimulate or move them in an effort to find relief. Typically, a person with this problem will be lying in bed trying to get to sleep when his or her legs begin to feel uncomfortable. Moving or stimulating the legs relieves the sensation.

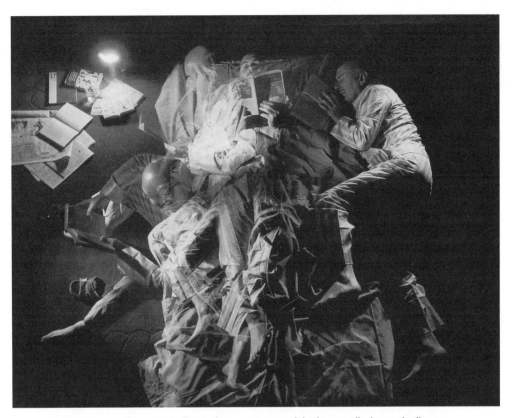

Restless legs syndrome typically involves movement of the legs to alleviate a tingling or prickly feeling. This multiple-exposure image shows a man's vain attempts to relieve the annoying sensations, punctuated by periods of reading as the problem prevents him from falling asleep.

Researchers estimate that between 3 and 8 percent of Americans suffer from RLS. Many of these people may have a mild form of the disorder, which causes few, infrequent, or moderate symptoms. However, for thousands of people, RLS severely affects their everyday lives. The movement in the leg is an extension of the big toe, but the ankle, the knee, and sometimes the hip are partly flexed as well. Each twitch can last from 1 to 3 seconds and can occur every 10 to 60 seconds. Typically an episode will last anywhere from a few minutes to several hours. In severe cases, it may go on all night.

The movements themselves seem to do no harm, and some heavy sleepers experience them with no problem. However, if the sensation is strong or if the person is a light sleeper, he or she may be awakened by

TEST FOR RESTLESS LEGS SYNDROME

If you answer "yes" to any of these questions, you should consider consulting a doctor:

- Does your bed partner complain that you kick during the night?
- Do you feel as though your sleep is not refreshing or restful?
- Do your legs ache before you go to bed or when you get up in the morning?

them. If the movements then cease, the individual may not know what awakened him or her. If the awakenings are frequent, they can result in excessive daytime sleepiness.

CAUSE

No one knows for certain what causes RLS, but scientists suspect that the causes are many. The problem is most likely to occur during periods of inactivity—not just when lying in bed but also while riding in a car, reading or watching television, or sitting in a movie theater. Sometimes the sensations are associated with medications—for example, certain tranquilizers and some high-blood-pressure, antinausea, antiseizure, and cold and allergy drugs—poor circulation, metabolic diseases, kidney ailments, or a folic acid deficiency. For more than 30 years, scientists have been aware that anemia and low levels of iron in the blood are associated with symptoms of RLS. Chronic conditions such as diabetes, peripheral neuropathy (damage to the nerves in the hands and feet), alcoholism, Parkinson's disease, kidney failure, and rheumatoid arthritis may trigger longer-lasting RLS symptoms.

New research also suggests a connection between RLS and symptoms of attention-deficit/hyperactivity disorder (a psychological disorder seen mainly in children and adolescents characterized by prominent symptoms of inattention and/or impulsivity).

Drinking caffeine-containing beverages, such as coffee, tea, hot chocolate, and soft drinks may trigger symptoms. Removing caffeine from the diet will usually decrease or eliminate the problem. Alcohol can also aggravate the condition.

Up to 15 percent of pregnant women develop RLS symptoms, particularly during the last few months of pregnancy. Symptoms typically vanish after delivery.

RLS can be inherited—children born to a parent with this problem have a significantly increased risk of developing the disorder. The condition is not sex linked, which means that the genetic form of RLS occurs in the same proportion among boys and girls.

RLS can also occur when no family history of the condition is present and no underlying or associated conditions exist.

SYMPTOMS

Annoying (but painless) sensations in the legs produce an irresistible urge to move. The feelings have been described as crawling, tingling, prickling, creeping, burning, itching, pulling, and tugging. The sensations, which are not like pins and needles or numbness, also occasionally occur in the arms.

Symptoms usually appear (or get worse) only during rest and often lessen or disappear during movement. They increase in the evening and at night, especially when the individual is lying down. Because the symptoms tend to worsen at night, the sensations and the urge to move the legs can make it hard for the sufferer to fall asleep. This can cause the person to feel abnormally sleepy during the day. Eventually, chronic sleep deprivation and daytime sleepiness may interfere with school and work and may lead to mood swings and problems with personal relationships.

DIAGNOSIS

Although RLS is often diagnosed in people between the ages of 50 and 60, the symptoms typically appear much earlier. Often people have the disorder for many years before it is diagnosed and treated. Many individuals with RLS, particularly those with the genetic form of the disorder, can trace their symptoms to childhood, when the problem may have been labeled as simply growing pains or—because of the constant movement and fidgeting—as hyperactivity.

Because RLS has such classic symptoms, the disorder is most often diagnosed on the basis of medical history. After ruling out other medical conditions, a doctor can usually diagnose RLS from a description of the sensations. Three conditions are especially typical of the problem:

- Inactivity aggravates the symptoms.
- Inescapable urges to move the legs develop.
- Movement of the legs alleviates the symptoms.

There are no laboratory tests to confirm an RLS diagnosis, but a thorough exam and medical tests can reveal disorders such as iron deficiency that can be associated with RLS. For some people an overnight sleep test may help determine other causes of the disturbance.

TREATMENT

Any underlying medical conditions should be addressed before trying to treat symptoms of RLS. If an iron or vitamin deficiency is causing restless legs, supplementing with iron, vitamin B_{12}, or folate may be enough to ease symptoms. Because the use of even moderate amounts of some minerals (such as iron and calcium) can interfere with the body's ability to use other minerals, these supplements should be used only with a doctor's advice.

Walking or stretching, taking a hot or cold bath, massaging or using vibration on the legs, or practicing relaxation techniques can sometimes relieve symptoms. It's important to try to determine which habits and activities worsen the symptoms and which ones improve them. A healthy balanced diet, with vitamin supplementation as necessary, is beneficial. It is best to avoid all caffeine-containing products, including chocolate and caffeinated beverages such as coffee, tea, and soft drinks.

Unfortunately, many cases of RLS do not respond to the treatment of underlying disorders and the implementation of lifestyle changes. In these situations, medication may be needed. Although the U.S. Food and Drug Administration has not approved any drugs for the treatment of RLS, several different classes of medications are being studied and may be prescribed to treat the condition. Many patients report that a combination of drugs works best for them. But some find that a medication that has worked for an extended period of time suddenly ceases to do the job and must be substituted with another drug. Often doctors must try different medications to find the best drug and the best dosage for a particular individual.

HOW TO LIVE WITH
RESTLESS LEGS SYNDROME

The following tips can help alleviate some of the symptoms of RLS:

- Allow for frequent stops when traveling.
- Don't fight the urge to move. This can aggravate the symptoms.
- Elevate your desktop to a height that will allow you to stand while you work or read.
- Get out of bed. Find an activity that takes your mind off of your legs.
- Keep a sleep diary. If you find it difficult to sit and write, dictate into a small tape recorder.
- Keep track of the things that do and don't work, and share this information with your health care provider.
- Occupy your mind. Concentrating on an activity can prevent or relieve the symptoms of RLS.
- Share information about RLS with family and friends.

PERIODIC LIMB MOVEMENTS

Periodic limb movements syndrome (PLMS), also called sleep myoclonus, is a variation of RLS. The condition is characterized by brief, recurrent jerks of the ankles, knees, or arms. According to the *American Psychiatric Press Textbook of Psychiatry*, these movements usually occur every 20 to 40 seconds during sleep and extend rhythmically from the big toe and involve an upward bending of the ankle, knee, or hip. Some people experience 100 or more jerks each hour.

The movements usually do not occur continuously throughout the night. Typically, they take place during the first half of the night, during non-REM sleep. During REM (dreaming) sleep, they generally stop, probably because the muscles are normally paralyzed during REM sleep. The movements have also been associated with awakening from sleep. The individual may awaken completely or move into a lighter sleep.

The sleeping person is often unaware that he or she has PLMS. It is usually the sleep partner—who feels the kicking and motion in bed—who reports the problem. Even without the sufferer's conscious awareness, however, the movements disrupt the sleep. Therefore, people with PLMS may feel extremely tired during the day. About 80 percent of those who suffer from RLS also suffer from PLMS. Conversely, however, most people with PLMS (especially the elderly) do not report other features of RLS.

CAUSE

Although there is no known cause for PLMS, it is often seen in people with renal failure or iron deficiency and in pregnant women. The condition has also been associated with the use of certain medications, such as antidepressants, and with withdrawal from (discontinuation of the use of) other medications, such as anticonvulsants, benzodiazepines (tranquilizers), and sleeping pills. PLMS has a strong genetic component. About one out of every three sufferers reports a family history of this disorder.

SYMPTOMS

People with PLMS complain of a variety of symptoms in addition to the leg, knee, and arm movements—including difficulty falling asleep, trouble staying asleep, and excessive daytime sleepiness. Difficulty falling asleep may be confused with periods when an individual is awakened by limb movements that occur immediately after he or she has fallen asleep. Problems staying asleep may result from sleep movements combined with very brief awakenings throughout the night, which can create an overall feeling of lack of rest. The person may have only a mild complaint of unrefreshing sleep, or—even if the individual is unaware of any nighttime disturbance—he or she may experience extreme sleepiness during the day.

DIAGNOSIS

Although RLS can usually be diagnosed by the history alone, PLMS is best diagnosed by formal sleep studies. Almost everyone occasionally experiences a leg jerk during sleep. PLMS is not diagnosed unless the leg movements occur five or more times during each hour of sleep.

TREATMENT

Because it is not known what causes PLMS, doctors focus on treating the symptoms. Avoiding caffeine (coffee, chocolate, sodas, tea), alcohol, and nicotine can help. Discontinuing the use of certain medications can be beneficial. And correcting underlying medical disorders, such as diabetes and iron deficiency, sometimes alleviates the problem.

When the condition is severe enough, it may require medication, including benzodiazepines (although recall that withdrawal from such drugs can aggravate the problem), codeine, morphine, and methadone. Recently, medication used for Parkinson's disease has shown positive results in some people with PLMS. However, the response to medications varies greatly from person to person.

REM SLEEP BEHAVIOR DISORDER (ACTING OUT DREAMS)

REM sleep behavior disorder is characterized by sleep movements that attempt to act out dreams. This behavior can occur only occasionally or several times a night on successive nights. Some individuals with this condition exhibit violent behavior during sleep, which can cause their own or a bed partner's injury. The person may punch, kick, leap out of bed, or even run from the bed during an attempted dream enactment. The condition can begin at any age but is most common in adult males.

CAUSE

There is usually no obvious cause for this problem. Occasionally, it has been seen as a side effect of withdrawal from alcohol, sedatives, or antidepressants. Sometimes the condition is associated with brain disorders, such as dementia or stroke.

TREATMENT

If frequent violent behavior occurs, treatment may be needed. A medication called chlormarzipan (a tranquilizer) has been found to be effective.

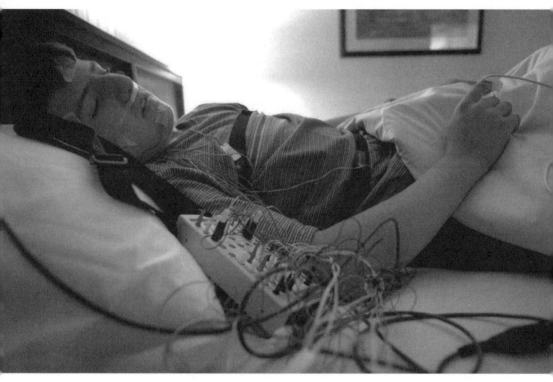

The diagnosis of breathing-related sleep problems usually involves polysomnography. This young man is being tested at the National Sleep Foundation in Stevens, Pennsylvania.

6

BREATHING-RELATED SLEEP PROBLEMS

Breathing-related sleep problems range from the fairly harmless condition of simple snoring to a potentially life-threatening disorder known as sleep apnea. For people with breathing-related sleep conditions, sleep disruption—caused by frequent awakening throughout the night as the person tries to breathe normally—can lead to excessive sleepiness or to insomnia. Chest discomfort, excessive body movement, and restlessness sometimes accompany breathing-related sleep problems, which can add to the person's difficulty sleeping.

Other symptoms of breathing-related sleep conditions include the following:

- confusion
- difficulty breathing when lying down or sleeping
- dry mouth
- excessive nighttime urination
- inappropriate behavior after sleep
- sleep drunkenness (the inability to awaken fully)

Children with breathing-related sleep disorders sometimes exhibit daytime mouth breathing, difficulty swallowing, and poor speech articulation. They may also develop learning disabilities. Unusual sleeping postures, such as sleeping on the hands and knees, occur more often in youngsters with these conditions.

According to the *DSM-IV*, between 1 and 10 percent of adults suffer from breathing-related sleep disorders. Although these problems can strike at any time in life, most people seek treatment between the ages of 40 and 60. Women are more likely to seek treatment following menopause. Although

One of the symptoms of breathing-related sleep problems is sleep drunkenness. This groggy woman with half-closed eyes shows the typical signs of this inability to fully awaken.

men outnumber women patients eight to one, boys and girls have an equal chance of developing this disorder.

SNORING

Snoring is one of the most common sleep problems. Just about everyone knows someone who snores—a parent, a grandparent, or a relative. Often, we tease the family snorer relentlessly about his or her bedroom decibel level, but snoring can sometimes be a serious matter.

Snoring refers to the noise that's produced when we breathe (usually while inhaling) during sleep. As we breathe in, the air vibrates the soft palate and uvula (the little piece of tissue hanging down in the back of the throat). Every snorer has at least some blockage of the upper airway—that blockage is what causes the noise. This type of snoring, also known as primary (or simple) snoring, refers to loud airway breathing sounds that do not involve any episodes of nonbreathing during sleep.

Some snorers, however, have a more serious problem: they suffer from sleep apnea—periods during which their airways are completely blocked (usually for at least 10 seconds at a time). The silence of this cessation of breathing is followed by a snort or gasp as the sleeper struggles to take a breath. When snoring is so loud that the noise disturbs others in the house, the problem may be connected with sleep apnea.

SYMPTOMS

A person who experiences simple snoring that is not associated with other breathing problems is typically characterized by the following:

- no complaints from others about the snoring
- no evidence of excessive sleepiness during the day
- no evidence of insomnia

In these cases, tests during snoring sleep will reveal normal sleeping and breathing patterns, no signs of other sleep problems, and no corresponding abrupt episodes of awakening.

TREATMENT

Because snoring is sometimes related to obesity, weight loss may be recommended. Sleeping on the side, rather than face up or face down, can also help relieve snoring. Alcohol and sedatives, which can aggravate snoring, should be avoided. In addition, there are devices on the market that can be worn in the mouth to keep the airway open. Some mechanisms bring the jaw forward, or elevate the soft palate, or keep the tongue from falling back and blocking the air passage. In more severe cases, surgery can remove excess tissue from the throat.

SLEEP APNEA

Sleep apnea, or episodes of breathing failure during sleep, can cause serious problems and can even be fatal. During sleep apnea (known medically as obstructive sleep apnea syndrome), a person has recurring periods of obstruction in the upper airway during sleep. Sometimes, as the airway muscles relax and collapse during sleep, the upper airway is

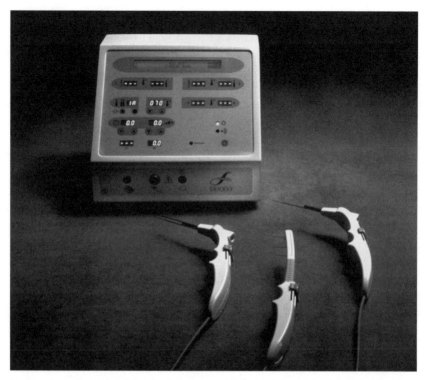

Snoring is produced by blockage of the upper airway. Various mechanisms, such as the antisnoring machine shown here, have been devised to prevent the condition by keeping the passageway open.

blocked by excess tissue (such as swollen tonsils or an enlarged tongue). The nasal passages can also become blocked. Occasionally, the structure of the jaw and the airway themselves can contribute to sleep apnea.

A rarer form of sleep apnea, called central sleep apnea, involves the cessation of breathing as a result of a neuromuscular problem.

SYMPTOMS

People with sleep apnea are usually not aware that they stop breathing during the night. However, individuals with this condition typically share the following symptoms:

- depression
- difficulty concentrating
- dry mouth after awakening
- excessive perspiration

- excessive sleepiness during the day
- frequent nighttime urination
- heartburn
- high blood pressure
- insomnia
- loud snoring
- morning headaches
- obesity
- restless sleep

DIAGNOSIS

A doctor can diagnose sleep apnea through polysomnography. This test, which can be given either at home or at a special sleep center, measures brain waves, muscle tension, eye movement, breathing, the oxygen level in the blood, and auditory sounds (such as gasping and snoring).

RISKS

Sleep apnea is a potentially life-threatening problem. If left untreated, it can lead to heart attacks, heart disease, high blood pressure, impotence, irregular heartbeat, or strokes.

DO YOU HAVE SLEEP APNEA?

Some people who snore also suffer from sleep apnea. If you answer "yes" to any of these questions, you should consider seeking medical help:

- Are you overweight?
- Do you feel groggy or sleepy when you wake up?
- Do you feel sleepy during the day?
- Has anyone ever noticed you choking, gasping, or holding your breath during sleep?
- Is your snoring loud and long, annoying others in the house?

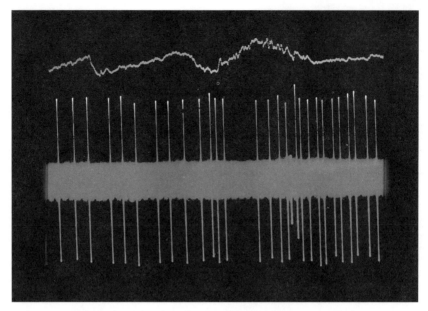

Polysomnography to determine the existence of sleep apnea measures brain waves, muscle tension, eye movement, breathing, the amount of oxygen in the blood, and sounds. The portion of the test shown here indicates brain waves (top) and eye movement (bottom).

TREATMENT

The treatment for mild sleep apnea can be as simple as changing certain behaviors—for example, losing weight and sleeping on one's side. Devices that fit into the mouth and keep the airway open can also be helpful. Sleep apnea that begins as a mild problem can become worse with age if left untreated.

For more severe cases, treatment may involve the use of a special machine that blows air into the nose through a mask to keep the airway open. Extreme cases may require a machine that blows air at two different pressures—a higher pressure when the person inhales and a lower pressure when the person exhales.

Surgical treatments may be appropriate for people with underlying physical problems, such as an abnormally small jaw or an abnormally small opening at the back of the throat. Surgery may also be helpful for individuals with swollen tonsils, an enlarged tongue, or any other tissue that partially blocks the airway. Correction of a deviated septum to open the nasal passages may also be in order.

CASE HISTORY

In a 1996 article, Eric Nofzinger and Charles Reynolds reported the case of John, a 75-year-old man who sought medical help for restless sleep at night and exhaustion during the day.

John's symptoms had been getting progressively worse over the previous 10 years. He kept turning over problems in his mind and had trouble finding a comfortable position for his legs, frequently getting up and pacing from room to room in an attempt to relax. When he would finally fall asleep, he would be plagued by vivid dreams of his experiences as a prisoner during World War II. During sleep, he would snore loudly and twitch his legs. The following day, he would feel tired and listless, as if he "had been fighting throughout the night."

John's doctors discovered that he habitually stopped breathing hundreds of times during the night as his airway muscles collapsed, blocking his upper air passages. They prescribed a device that uses air pressure to keep the air passages open throughout the night. The mechanism almost entirely eliminated John's periods of sleep apnea. Because John still had trouble falling asleep, his doctors gave him a tranquilizing medication to ease his restless legs syndrome. Three years later, John's problems had almost completely disappeared.

Internal mechanisms that control our biological rhythms allow us to live in harmony with cycles of nature such as day and night. This abstract image represents the internal body clock that controls our sleeping and waking cycles.

7

SLEEP-WAKE RHYTHM DISTURBANCE

Recall from our discussion in chapter 1 that we all have an internal 25-hour biological clock, known as the circadian rhythm cycle, which is controlled by light and other sensory inputs such as temperature. The release of a hormone called melatonin in the brain, which occurs in response to darkness, is also believed to play a large part in controlling the body's circadian rhythm. Our internal sleep-wake rhythm roughly conforms to this 25-hour cycle. Although we all have a sleep-wake pattern, however, these patterns differ from one person to another.

"LARKS" AND "OWLS"

In any given population, because of the makeup of each person's body chemistry and internal circadian rhythm, some individuals are morning people ("larks") and others are night people ("owls"). The patterns of "larks" and "owls" may be not too far from "normal," or they may be quite unusual. If the mismatch is severe between a person's natural sleep-wake pattern and society's demands, problems can result. For example, most adults wake up at 6 A.M. and are in bed by 10 P.M. However, if a "lark" wants to start the day at 4 A.M., he or she may feel sleepy by 8 P.M. A "night owl" who does not want to get up before 9 A.M. may then stay up until midnight.

There is a small group of people whose natural tendency to fall asleep is delayed until long past midnight and who do not naturally awaken until noon. These individuals suffer from one of the most persistent types of sleep-wake rhythm problems: they have a delayed sleep-wake pattern, with their inner sleep-wake cycles running behind the demands of society. They seem to be able to stay up later than (and, consequently, do not get up as early as) others. They complain of problems falling asleep at a socially acceptable bedtime and rising at an early hour with the rest of the world. Because our circadian sleep cycles tend to be stable, when these people are left to their own schedules, most

Nocturnal individuals, such as the television-watching night owl in this illustration, have naturally later sleep-wake patterns than do morning people. If the patterns conflict with life's demands, difficulties can arise.

of them consistently fall asleep and wake up a few hours later than the average individual. People with this problem typically find it very hard to change their pattern. They often need multiple alarm clocks to awaken them, and they may become chronically fatigued when they are forced to follow society's sleep-wake pattern.

Researchers first identified this sleep-wake pattern disturbance in 1979. They explained that the problem can be attributed to the fact that, although a day on earth is 24 hours long, basic human circadian rhythm is based on a 25-hour cycle. The problem can also manifest itself as advanced sleep-wake pattern, in which an individual falls asleep in the early evening and spontaneously awakens before dawn. Each day, average people automatically reset their biological clocks to close the gap between the sun's 24-hour day and the body's 25-hour cycle. In fact, experts believe that Monday-morning blues are really mini–jet lags caused by keeping later weekend hours that require a circadian correction.

According to Anders and Eiben's article "Pediatric Sleep Disorders," the problem of delayed sleep-wake patterns often begins after prolonged periods of sleep deprivation and irregular hours. It's especially common among teenagers, who often sleep only six to seven hours on weekday nights and then stay up late on weekends. Some teens try to repay their sleep debt by sleeping later on weekends. Because alternating nights of little sleep with irregular periods of longer sleep disrupts the biological clock, however, these sleep patterns can be tolerated for only short amounts of time.

Delayed sleep-wake patterns have also been associated with the absence of time cues, such as exposure to sunlight. During winter in the polar latitudes, daylight may be too dim to set an individual's internal clock. Similarly, excessive use of sunglasses may throw off circadian rhythms.

In some cases, head trauma has altered sleep-wake patterns. Caffeine has also been linked to the problem, because it can lengthen the circadian period and delay sleep. Other substances, such as antidepressants, alcohol, certain asthma medications, and sedatives, may also affect circadian rhythms.

DIAGNOSIS

The diagnosis of delayed sleep-wake patterns is based on a person's history and on documentation through overnight sleep tests. Patients who keep sleep logs usually reveal 60- to 90-minute periods of insomnia at bedtime (which often begins past midnight). Once the circadian clock is disrupted, these altered patterns often persist even during periods, such as vacations, when the person should be able to get an adequate amount of sleep. Even in situations when bedtimes are strictly enforced (such as at overnight camps), teens with delayed sleep-wake patterns typically can't fall asleep until after midnight. This problem, which can last for months, years, or even decades, is extremely difficult to treat.

Interestingly, more young people claim to be "night owls" than any other age group. In a survey of 109 students, aged 12 to 19, 16 percent reported having chronic difficulty falling asleep and waking up. This problem has also been linked to a somewhat higher incidence of depression (in fact, late sleeping itself can trigger depression).

TREATMENT

The treatment of sleep-wake rhythm disturbance requires patience and support. The individual must generally keep diaries showing sleep-wake patterns and daily activities, work to manage stress and set priorities, and resolve to maintain regular bedtime and waking hours. In addition, some people have found it helpful to wear sunglasses in the afternoon but not in the morning. The use of bright lights in the morning can also be beneficial.

If behavioral treatment is unsuccessful, the individual can try to shift his or her sleep onset time. Coping with a delayed sleep-wake pattern has been described as rather like living on a one-way street and being unable to back up even one or two houses. The obvious solution is to drive around the block—or to progressively delay bedtimes and rising times until the desired schedule is found. Each day, the person delays sleep and wake times by one to two hours, in order to shift the sleep onset time, around the clock, to a more appropriate hour. When a 10 P.M. to 11 P.M. bedtime is achieved, the therapy is stopped.

Advancing the biological clock has also proven successful with teenagers. This procedure involves having the teen go to bed 15 minutes earlier every few days until he or she reaches the desired sleep onset time. Weekly improvements are sometimes no more than 15 to 30 minutes. Once the teenager achieves the change in sleeping pattern, he or she must strictly adhere to the new schedule to prevent the delayed sleep rhythm from returning.

JET LAG

Jet lag occurs when there is any kind of disturbance in the body's circadian rhythm, producing physical and mental stress. The name comes from the disruption that occurs in the body's internal clock when we cross several time zones in an airplane. But the problem—sometimes referred to as industrial jet lag or night-shift problems—can also occur when a person switches from day-shift to night-shift work.

Flying from one time zone to another can bring a person into conflict with his or her own circadian rhythm. The severity of the problem depends on the number of time zones crossed. Traveling through eight or more time zones in under 24 hours has proven most troublesome.

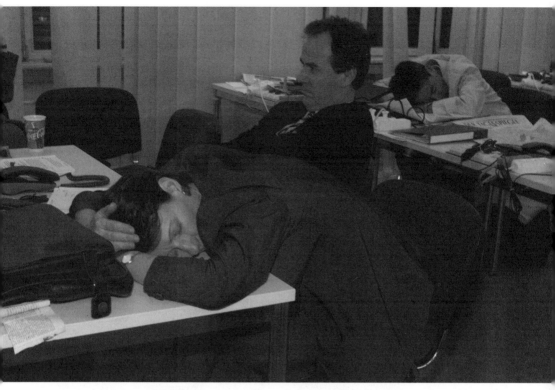

Changing time zones can throw a person's circadian rhythm out of whack. These journalists sleep at a press center after traveling from near and far to attend an international summit.

Eastward travel—which requires setting sleep-wake patterns ahead—is typically more difficult for people to tolerate than is westward travel. Individuals who begin their trip excited, stressed, tired, or ill also have an increased risk of these problems.

A person with jet lag will typically feel drowsy, lethargic, and fatigued. The individual may struggle with insomnia, poor concentration and motivation, and slowed thinking for a number of days. The person may find it hard to get anything done; may feel hungry and thirsty at odd hours; and may suffer from moodiness, headaches, and muscle aches. Research has shown that it takes about one day per time zone crossed to readjust the circadian rhythm.

Fortunately, there are a number of measures that can be taken before a trip in order to prevent jet lag. Here are some important steps to follow:

1. Stay relaxed, well rested, and stress free before boarding the airplane. (Get plenty of rest the night before.)

2. Take a nonstop, daytime flight, if possible.

3. If your flight takes place during the hours that will be your sleep time at your destination, try to sleep during those hours. (For example, if you fly from San Francisco to London, arriving in the early morning, you will be flying during London's late night hours, and you should try to sleep on the plane.)

4. Bring blindfolds, neck rests, and blow-up pillows to ensure that you will have quality rest on the airplane.

5. Walk around the airplane and stretch in your seat to reduce leg swelling.

Working rotating-shift schedules can sometimes lead to chronic sleep problems. This man's schedule, which requires that he work afternoons from Monday through Thursday and switch to a day shift on Friday and Sunday, gives his body little opportunity to adjust to the changes.

6. When you arrive, expose yourself to natural light (but not direct sunlight) to resynchronize your internal time clock.

7. Avoid sleeping during the day at your destination.

SHIFT WORK

Some sleep problems occur when individuals work shifts that disrupt the body's internal circadian rhythm, which results in sleep loss. These workers find themselves on the job when their bodies are telling them that they should be asleep. According to the National Institute of Occupational Safety and Health, more than 5 million Americans work such shifts.

When the normal sleep-wake pattern is disrupted, night-shift workers—who must try to sleep during the day when their body clocks are telling them that they should be awake—may find that they cannot sleep. Insufficient sleep can also result from daytime social and family demands and from daytime environmental disturbances, such as ringing telephones and traffic noises, which can interrupt scheduled sleep time.

Rotating-shift schedules, which not only force workers to adopt abnormal circadian rhythms but also prevent them from being able to make consistent adjustments, are the most troublesome of all. Night-shift and rotating-shift workers typically sleep for shorter periods of time and wake up more often than daytime workers do. This pattern naturally causes sleep loss, which then results in excessive sleepiness. This sleepiness can cause problems on the job. Some experts believe that extensive shift work can lead to chronic sleep disturbance.

When they can, night-shift and rotational-shift employees should consider changing their schedules, including switching from permanent night shifts and avoiding quick shift changes. However, many people who work nontraditional shifts have little choice about their schedules. The individuals will need to establish a consistent sleep routine, make sure to get plenty of exercise, and maintain a good diet. They should also consider using bright lights to adjust their bodies' circadian rhythms and alter the time for their bodies' peak alertness.

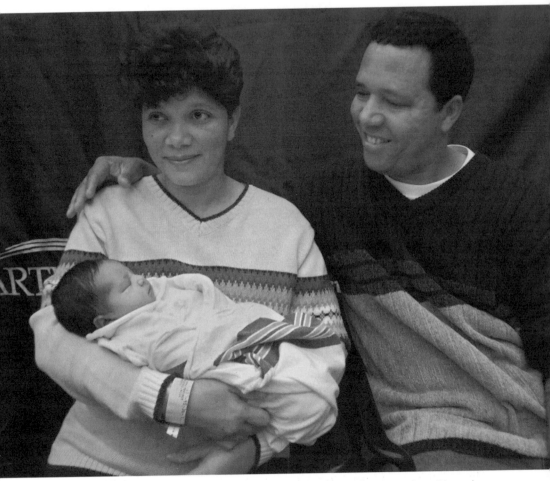

Sleep is a function that allows our bodies and minds to recharge. Infants, such as this newborn, who are rapidly growing and developing, are believed to use this time to test and adjust their body systems.

8

SLEEP: THE FINAL FRONTIER

A bnormalities in sleep help teach us about the role that normal slumber plays in our lives. Gradually, the function of sleep as replenishing neurotransmitters (chemical substances that transmit impulses between nerves), conserving energy, and processing information is revealing its secrets to researchers.

We still wonder, however, why the human fetus spends up to 80 percent of its time in REM sleep. One answer seems to be that the ability to activate eye and body movements during dream sleep allows the developing organism to test and refine its circuitry.

With respect to our mental processes, sleep is essential for both remembering and forgetting. According to *Sleep*, by J. Allan Hobson, it is widely believed that, in order for information to be permanently stored in the brain, it must be converted from electrical activity into the brain's neuron structure—a process that takes place during sleep. Some microbiologists believe that, in order for memory to be maintained, it must be constantly renewed. Other scientists theorize that, in order to prevent the loss of memory, REM sleep must remove undesirable data. In other words, if we remembered every piece of information our brains ever absorbed, there would soon be no room for new information. It is possible that sleep allows us to eliminate useless data and reinforce critical data.

Dreams may be difficult to remember precisely because they were designed to be erased automatically and because they activate a system that discards unwanted information. Although dreams may be considered expendable, it seems clear that they represent an important connection to the imagination. And the presence of chemicals in the brain that trigger hallucinations (during sleep or wakefulness) leads to the question of whether creativity and delusional images may be linked in some fashion. The ability to perceive things that aren't there can be either a sign of insanity or a sign of genius. In order to formulate new inventions, after all, we must be capable of seeing beyond the limits of the physical world.

Sleep is one of the last frontiers of consciousness that scientists have begun to explore. It is becoming increasingly clear that the study of sleep is essential in the research of brain function. "Beneath its cloak of outward calm," Hobson observes, "sleep conceals a rich array of dynamic processes." We are only now beginning to appreciate the complexity of its riches.

APPENDIX

FOR MORE INFORMATION

For more information about sleep problems and disorders, contact the following groups and organizations.

American Academy of Sleep Medicine (AASM)
6301 Bandel Road, Suite 101
Rochester, MN 55901
(507) 287-6006
http://www.aasmnet.org

American Psychiatric Association
1400 K Street NW
Washington, DC 20005
(202) 682-6000
http://www.psych.org

American Psychological Association (APA)
750 First Street NE
Washington, DC 20002
(202) 336-5500
http://www.apa.org

American Sleep Apnea Association
1424 K Street NW, Suite 302
Washington, DC 20005
(202) 293-3650
http://www.sleepapnea.org

Narcolepsy and Sleep Disorders Online Newsletter
http://www.narcolepsy.com

Narcolepsy Network
10921 Reed Hartman Highway
Cincinnati, OH 45242
(513) 891-3522
http://www.websciences.org

National Institute of Mental Health (NIMH)
NIMH Public Inquiries
6001 Executive Boulevard
Room 8184, MSC 9663
Bethesda, MD 20892-9663
(301) 443-4513
E-mail: nimhinfo@nih.gov
http://www.nimh.nih.gov

National Mental Health Association (NMHA)
1021 Prince Street
Alexandria, VA 22314-2971
(703) 684-7722
(800) 969-6642
http://www.nmha.org

Restless Legs Syndrome (RLS) Foundation
P.O. Box 7050, Dept WWW
Rochester, MN 55902-2985
http://www/.rls.org

Alvarez, A. *Night: Night Life, Night Language, Sleep and Dreams.* New York: W. W. Norton, 1995.

American Psychiatric Association. *Diagnostic and Statistical Manual of Mental Disorders.* 4th ed. Washington, D.C.: American Psychiatric Association, 1994.

Anders, Thomas, and Lisa Eiben. "Pediatric Sleep Disorders: A Review of the Past 10 Years." *Journal of the American Academy of Child and Adolescent Psychiatry* 36, no. 1 (1997).

Andreev, B. V. *Sleep Therapy in the Neuroses.* New York: Consultants Bureau, 1960.

Arkin, Arthur. *Sleep-Talking: Psychology and Psychophysiology.* Hillsdale, N.J., 1981.

Arnason, H. H. *History of Modern Art, Painting, and Sculpture.* New York: Harry N. Abrams, 1986.

Bell, C. C., et al. "Prevalence of Isolated Sleep Paralysis in Black Subjects." *Journal of the National Medical Association* 76, no. 3/4 (1984): 501.

Billiard, M., A. Besset, and J. Cadilhac. "The Clinical and Polygraphic Development of Narcolepsy." In *Sleep/Wake Disorders: Natural History, Epidemiology, and Long-Term Evolution.* Ed. C. Guilleminault and E. Lugaresi. New York: Raven Press, 1983.

Binns, E. *The Anatomy of Sleep or the Art of Procuring Sound and Refreshing Slumber at Will.* London: John Churchill, 1842.

Breger, Louis, Ian Hunter, and Ron Lane. *The Effects of Stress on Dreams.* New York: International Universities Press, 1971.

Buysse, Daniel, et al. "Diagnostic Concordance for *DSM-IV* Sleep Disorders." *American Journal of Psychiatry* 151, no. 9 (1994).

Coren, Stanley. *Sleep Thieves: An Eye-Opening Exploration into the Science and Mysteries of Sleep.* New York: Free Press, 1996.

Davison, Gerald, and John Neale. *Abnormal Psychology: An Experimental Clinical Approach.* New York: John Wiley and Sons, 1982.

Empson, Jacob. *Sleep and Dreaming.* New York: Harvester Wheatsheaf, 1993.

Everett, H. C. "Sleep Paralysis in Medical Students." *Journal of Nervous Mental Disorders* 136, no. 3/4 (1963): 283.

Flemming, William. *Arts and Ideas.* New York: Holt, Reinhart, and Winston, 1963.

Freud, Sigmund. *The Interpretation of Dreams: Standard Edition of the Complete Psychological Works of Sigmund Freud.* Vol. 4. Ed. and trans. J. Strachey. London: Hogarth Press, 1960.

Fukuda, K. et al. "High Prevalence of Isolated Sleep Paralysis: Kanashebari Phenomenon in Japan." *Sleep* 10, no. 3/4 (1987): 279.

Gackenbach, Jayne, and Stephen Laberge. *Conscious Mind, Sleeping Brain: Perspectives on Lucid Dreaming.* New York: Plenum Press, 1988.

Gaillard, J. M. "Neurotransmitters and Sleep Pharmacology." In *Handbook of Sleep Disorders.* Ed. M. J. Thorpy. New York: Marcel Dekker, 1990.

Ghaemi, Nassir, and Michael Irizarry. "Parasomnias as Neuropsychiatric Complications of Electrical Injury." *Psychosomatics* 36, no. 4 (1995).

Goode, G. B. "Sleep Paralysis." *Archive of Neurology* 6, no. 3/4 (1962): 68.

Goodman, W. K., et al. "The Yale-Brown Obsessive Compulsive Scale: II. Validity." *Archive of General Psychiatry* 46, no. 3/4 (1989): 1012.

Hales, Robert E., Stuart C. Yudofsky, and John A. Talbott, eds. *American Psychiatric Press Textbook of Psychiatry,* 2nd ed. Washington, D.C.: American Psychiatric Press, 1994.

Hall, Bolton. *The Psychology of Sleep.* New York: Moffat, Yard, 1916.

Hammond, William. *Sleep and Its Derangements.* New York: Da Capo Press, 1982.

Hartmann, Ernest. *The Nightmare: The Psychology and Biology of Terrifying Dreams.* New York: Basic Books, 1984.

Hishikawa, Y. "Sleep Paralysis." In *Narcolepsy: Proceedings of the First International Symposium on Narcolepsy.* Ed. C. Guilleminault, W. C. Dement, and P. Passouant. New York: Spectrum, 1976.

Hobson, J. Allan. *Sleep.* New York: Scientific American Library, 1989.

Hufford, David J. *The Terror That Comes in the Night.* Philadelphia: University of Pennsylvania Press, 1982.

Jung, Carl. *Dreams*. Princeton, N.J.: Princeton University Press, 1974.

Kavey, Neil, and Jamie White. "Somnambulism Associated with Hallucinations." *Psychosomatics* 34, no. 1 (1993).

Kellerman, Henry, ed. *The Nightmare: Psychological and Biological Foundations*. New York: Columbia University Press, 1986.

Kellner, Robert, et al. "Changes in Chronic Nightmares After One Session of Desensitization or Rehearsal Instructions." *American Journal of Psychiatry* 149, no. 5 (1992).

Kline, Milton, ed. *Clinical Correlations of Experimental Hypnosis*. Springfield, Ill.: Charles C Thomas, 1963.

Koran, Lorrin, and Sharadha Raghavan. "Fluoxetine for Isolated Sleep Paralysis." *Psychosomatics* 34, no. 2 (1993).

Kraft-Ebing, R. Von. *An Experimental Study in the Domain of Hypnotism*. New York: Da Capo Press, 1982.

Kramer, Kenneth Paul. *Death Dreams: Unveiling Mysteries of the Unconscious Mind*. New York: Paulist Press, 1993.

Langdon, N., et al. "Fluoxetine in the Treatment of Cataplexy." *Sleep* 9, no. 3/4 (1986): 371.

London, Perry. *Beginning Psychology*. Homewood, Ill.: Dorsey Press, 1978.

McCall, W. Vaughn. "Management of Primary Sleep Disorders Among Elderly Persons." *Psychosomatics* 46, no. 1 (1995).

Milby, Jesse, et al. "Effectiveness of Combined Triazolam-Behavioral Therapy for Primary Insomnia." *American Journal of Psychiatry* 150, no. 8 (1993).

Mitchell, S. W. "On Some Disorders of Sleep." *Virginia Medical Journal* 2, no. 3/4 (1876): 769.

Moorcroft, William. *Sleep, Dreaming, and Sleep Disorders*. New York: University Press of America, 1993.

Nofzinger, Eric, and Charles Reynolds. "Sleep Impairment and Daytime Sleepiness in Later Life." *American Journal of Psychiatry* 153, no. 7 (1996).

Ogilvie, Robert, and John Hash. *Sleep Onset: Normal and Abnormal Processes*. Washington, D.C.: American Psychological Association, 1994.

Ohaeri, J. U., et al. "The Pattern of Isolated Sleep Among Nigerian Medical Students." *Journal of the National Medical Association* 81, no. 3/4 (1989): 805.

Oren, Dan, et al. *How to Beat Jet Lag*. New York: Henry Holt, 1993.

Owley, Thomas, and Joseph Flaherty. "New-Onset Narcolepsy and Paroxetine." *Psychosomatics* 35, no. 6 (1994).

Penn, N. E., D. R. Kripke, and J. Scharff. "Sleep Paralysis Among Medical Students." *Journal of Psychology* 107, no. 3/4 (1981): 247.

Regestein, Quentin, et al. "Daytime Alertness in Patients with Primary Insomnia." *American Journal of Psychiatry* 150, no. 10 (October 1993).

Regestein, Quentin, and Timothy Monk. "Delayed Sleep Phase Syndrome: A Review of Its Clinical Aspects." *American Journal of Psychiatry* 152, no. 4 (1995).

Rubinstein, Hilary. *Insomniacs of the World, Goodnight.* New York: Random House, 1974.

Salin-Pascual, Rafael, et al. "Long-term Study of the Sleep of Insomnia Patients with Sleep State Misperception and Other Insomnia Patients." *American Journal of Psychiatry* 149, no. 7 (1992).

Schramm, Elizabeth, et al. "The Structured Interview for Sleep Disorders According to *DSM-III-R.*" *American Journal of Psychiatry* 150, no. 6 (1993).

Sloane, Paul. *Psychoanalytic Understanding of the Dream.* New York: Jason Aronson, 1979.

Torczyner, Harry. *Magritte: Ideas and Images.* New York: Harry N. Abrams, 1966.

APPENDIX

FURTHER READING

Ancoli-Israel, Sonia. *All I Want Is a Good Night's Sleep*. Philadelphia: Mosby, 1996.

Ball, Nigel, and Nick Hough. *The Sleep Solution: A 21-Night Program to Better Sleep*. New York: Ulysses Press, 1998.

Bruno, Frank Joe. *Get a Good Night's Sleep: Understand Your Sleeplessness— And Banish It Forever!* New York: IDG Books, 1997.

Buchman, Dian Dincin, and Don R. Bensen, eds. *The Complete Guide to Natural Sleep*. New York: Keats Publishing, 1997.

Dement, William C., and Christopher Vaughan. *The Promise of Sleep: A Pioneer in Sleep Medicine Explains the Vital Connection Between Health, Happiness, and a Good Night's Sleep*. New York: Delacorte Press, 1999.

Inlander, Charles B., and Cynthia K. Moran. *Sixty-seven Ways to Good Sleep: A People's Medical Society Book*. New York: Walker, 1995.

Jacobs, Gregg D. *Say Good Night to Insomnia*. New York: Henry Holt, 1999.

Moore, Martin. *The Complete Idiot's Guide to Getting a Good Night's Sleep*. New York: Macmillan, 1998.

Simpson, Carolyn. *Coping with Sleep Disorders*. New York: Rosen Publishing, 1996.

Wiedman, John. *Desperately Seeking Snoozin': The Insomnia Cure from Awake to Zzzzz*. Towering Pines Press, 1999.

APPENDIX

GLOSSARY

Apnea: periodic cessation of breathing, especially during sleep.

Behavioral therapy: a form of therapy that uses reinforcement to promote desirable behaviors and discourage undesirable behaviors.

Bruxism: the habit of unconsciously grinding or clenching the teeth, especially in situations of stress or during sleep.

Cataplexy: sudden loss of muscle power, sometimes triggered by a strong emotion.

Electroencephalograph (EEG): a machine that measures electrical activity in the brain.

Hallucination: a sensory perception, usually involving sight, hearing, or smell, in which a person imagines that something is real when it is not.

Hypersomnia: a type of sleep disorder in which the person can't seem to get enough sleep.

Insomnia: the inability to fall or stay asleep or the inability to sleep restfully.

Narcolepsy: a serious form of hypersomnia characterized by irresistible urges to sleep during the day, hallucinations, and sleep paralysis.

Periodic limb movements syndrome (PLMS): a condition characterized by brief, recurrent jerks of the ankles, knees, or arms.

Polysomnography: a test that monitors sleep through the measurement of EEG activity.

REM (rapid eye movement) sleep: a state of sleep that occurs during dreaming and rapid eye movements and that recurs several times during a normal period of sleep.

REM sleep behavior disorder: a condition characterized by sleep movements that attempt to act out dreams.

Restless legs syndrome (RLS): a condition characterized by a crawling, tingling, or prickling sensation in the legs that prompts a strong urge to move or stimulate the legs in order to relieve the sensation.

Sleep paralysis: the inability to move shortly after awakening or shortly after dozing off.

APPENDIX

INDEX

APPENDIX

PICTURE CREDITS

Senior Consulting Editor Carol C. Nadelson, M.D., is president and chief executive officer of the American Psychiatric Press, Inc., staff physician at Cambridge Hospital, and Clinical Professor of Psychiatry at Harvard Medical School. In addition to her work with the American Psychiatric Association, which she served as vice president in 1981–83 and president in 1985–86, Dr. Nadelson has been actively involved in other major psychiatric organizations, including the Group for the Advancement of Psychiatry, the American College of Psychiatrists, the Association for Academic Psychiatry, the American Association of Directors of Psychiatric Residency Training Programs, the American Psychosomatic Society, and the American College of Mental Health Administrators. In addition, she has been a consultant to the Psychiatric Education Branch of the National Institute of Mental Health and has served on the editorial boards of several journals. Doctor Nadelson has received many awards, including the Gold Medal Award for significant and ongoing contributions in the field of psychiatry, the Elizabeth Blackwell Award for contributions to the causes of women in medicine, and the Distinguished Service Award from the American College of Psychiatrists for outstanding achievements and leadership in the field of psychiatry.

Consulting Editor Claire E. Reinburg, M.A., is editorial director of the American Psychiatric Press, Inc., which publishes about 60 new books and six journals a year. She is a graduate of Georgetown University in Washington, D.C., where she earned bachelor of arts and master of arts degrees in English. She is a member of the Council of Biology Editors, the Women's National Book Association, the Society for Scholarly Publishing, and Washington Book Publishers.

Linda Bayer, Ph.D., graduated from Boston University and received a master's degree in English from Clark University and a Ph.D. in humanities (English and art history). She later earned a master's degree in psychology from Harvard University and all clinical training and course work for a doctorate in education (counseling and consulting psychology)0. She worked with patients suffering from substance abuse and other problems at a guidance center and in the Boston public school system. Bayer was also a high school teacher before joining the faculties of several universities, including Wesleyan University, Hartford College for Women, American University, Boston University, and the U.S. Naval Academy. At the Hebrew University in Israel, she occupied the Sam and Ayala Zacks Chair. Bayer has also worked as a newspaper editor and a syndicated columnist, winning a Simon Rockower Award for excellence in journalism. Her published works include *The Gothic Imagination, The Blessing and the Curse* (a novel), and several books on substance abuse, as well as five volumes in the ENCYCLOPEDIA OF PSYCHOLOGICAL DISORDERS. Bayer is currently a senior speechwriter and a strategic analyst at the White House. She is the mother of two children, Lev and Ilana.